'A deeply personal and [...] Advent, this book is a balm [...] us on a journey of music [...] layered depth that provides room for both questioning and a lasting hope.'
Arun Arora, Bishop of Kirkstall

'The quest for authenticity has been a hallmark of Guli's journey since she arrived in this country as a refugee forty years ago. She enters with tenderness the places "where beauty and pain reside together and where we encounter God." She has an extraordinary ability to hear the music not only of the soul but of the future, and emboldens us to dance to it today.'
Robert Atwell, former Bishop of Exeter

'This beautiful book is infused with explorations into identity, belonging, and worth – as any book to be read through Advent should be. The Advent desire to be touched back into life, a call to be drawn to the native tranquillity of the soul, is given a textual music here. To read it is to find yourself wanting to listen with a refreshed depth worthy of the gift of life.'
Mark Oakley, Dean of Southwark

'This is a very personal book of reflections on themes for Advent, and yet, at the same time, it makes space for each reader to enter into their own attention to the powerful, peaceful, challenging and joyful action of God in Christ. There are riches to be found in every chapter – books to follow up, writers and speakers to explore and, above all, music to listen to. There is nothing sentimental here, but there is fearless emotion and boundless hope.'

Jane Williams, McDonald Professor in Christian Theology at St Mellitus College

LISTENING TO THE MUSIC OF THE SOUL

THE ARCHBISHOP OF YORK'S ADVENT BOOK 2025

Guli Francis-Dehqani

spck

SPCK
First published in Great Britain in 2025

SPCK
Part of the SPCK Group
Studio 101
The Record Hall
16–16A Baldwin's Gardens
London EC1N 7RJ
www.spckpublishing.co.uk

EU GPSR Authorised Representative
LOGOS EUROPE, 9 rue Nicolas Poussin, 17000, La Rochelle, France
Email: Contact@logoseurope.eu

British Library Cataloguing-in-Publication Data
A catalogue record for this book is available from the British Library

ISBN 978–0–281–09133–1
eBook ISBN 978–0–281–09134–8

1 3 5 7 9 10 8 6 4 2

Typeset by Fakenham Prepress Solutions, Fakenham, Norfolk NR21 8NL
First printed in Great Britain by Clays Limited, Bungay, Suffolk

eBook by Fakenham Prepress Solutions, Fakenham, Norfolk NR21 8NL

Produced on paper from sustainable sources

For my husband Lee and our children
Gabriel Iraj, Eleanor Nargess and Simeon Omid

Dr Guli Francis-Dehqani is the first woman from a minority ethnic background to be ordained as an Anglican bishop in the UK. Formerly Bishop of Loughborough, she is now Bishop of Chelmsford, and in January 2021, was appointed the Lead Bishop for Housing for the Church of England. She has served as a member of the Lords Spiritual in the House of Lords since November 2021. In 2023, Guli played a prominent role in the Coronation, administering Holy Communion to the King and Queen. She is a regular contributor to BBC Radio 4's *Thought for the Day*.

Born in Iran, Guli's family left the country in the wake of the Iranian Revolution in 1980 when she was 13 years old, and to date she has been unable to return. Her husband Lee is also a priest and they have three adult children.

Contents

Foreword

The rhythm of the Church's year feels like a constant, as the familiar narrative of God's loving purposes unfolds and we absorb the music of the seasons. Yet, with each Advent, the seeming recapitulation is likely to feature startling new notes. In an unpredictable world, our circumstances are subject to change; the contexts in which we find ourselves can alter, and we may discern in the melodies and stories of Christmas, things that we have never heard before.

In this captivating book, Bishop Guli reflects on our shared experience of contemporary life, and on her deeply personal experience of growing up as a Christian in Iran, the persecution endured by her family, and her (continuing) exile. Relating her story to biblical narratives, she encourages us to seek to set the story of our own lives within the greater one of God's enduring love and purpose for salvation. In each chapter, we are invited to listen to a musical interpretation of its theme – such as flight or angels or hope – and we are given space to respond in a way that will be unique to each one of us.

Some of the music will be familiar, some less so, but every piece invites us to listen and find meaning, refreshment and encouragement in the rhythms that mark the heartbeat of God's work in our lives. In a culture in which we are expected to respond immediately and instinctively to each event or social media post, Advent is a time to step back and reflect, to allow ourselves to be caught up again in anticipation of the coming of Christ.

Listening to the Music of the Soul is a book to be read carefully, even reverentially, for its themes touch the inner person very deeply. In sharing of her own life so generously, Bishop Guli shows us how we can be open to God reaching out to lead us ever further into the mystery of God's being. May the Lord, when he comes, find us watching and waiting – and listening.

Stephen Cottrell
Archbishop of York

Introduction

'Listening to the music of the soul' may be a wonderfully evocative phrase, but what does it actually mean? What relevance does such an idea have to waking up on a wet Monday morning when you're already stressing about the challenges of the day/week/year ahead? As someone well familiar with everyday anxiety myself, I hope to assure you that as we listen to the music of the soul – in *any and all* circumstances – we can begin to find ourselves not only inhabiting our own lives more fully but enabling others to live more fully too.

In a metaphorical sense (we'll come to a more literal one shortly), listening to the music of the soul expresses the importance of connecting in a meaningful way with our innermost being. We all need to be reminded every so often to let go of the pressure to be something or someone we're not. It is much better to seek those things that are deepest in our heart and speak to us of who we really are; to ponder on the way we relate to the world, to God and to others.

The enduring melodies of faith

The quest for authenticity has always been important for me. It involves knowing what my roots are as an Iranian Christian, recognising the things that have shaped me, and remaining open to new ways of understanding and being.

Authenticity in faith is about engaging in a relationship with God that connects with our lived experiences and covers a vast expanse between certainty at one end and doubt at the other. In his book *The Enduring Melody*,[1] the late great Michael Mayne, one-time dean of Westminster Abbey, talks of discovering the enduring melodies of faith. These are truths that lie deep at the centre, around which other airs and harmonies dance and develop. In musical terms, these truths are the *cantus firmus*, the ground base, which remains unchanged while allowing for experiment, improvisation and transformation.

In Christian terms, the enduring melodies for me are about God's abiding love shown through the person of Jesus, and the vision of working towards a more just society on earth while waiting for that eternal kingdom beyond death.

Each of us must discover our own enduring melodies, the themes that sustain us through the complexities of life, when meaning and hope can be hard to find. How we understand and articulate such ideas is likely to change over time. Sometimes particular melodies may provide variety and richness, intertwining as they fade in and out. Some will be painful, in a minor key; others joyfully exuberant, in a major one. But through everything, in life and in faith, the music of the soul, the truly *authentic* melody, remains steadfast, anchoring all else, providing stability and meaning even in our darkest moments.

Music plays a part in this book in a more literal way too. Like most people, I grew up surrounded by music. I learned at an early age to love and appreciate it and not only for its own qualities or the pleasure it brings, though those are not to be underestimated. I find it fascinating that because music is experienced in real time, it can invoke in us different responses and emotions depending on the context in which we're hearing it, the mood we're in or the people who are with us. It also connects us to past memories, to loved ones, to happy and sad occasions. It reminds us that we are alive, and hearing unfamiliar music can fasten us to new memories, even as they are being created. In a very real sense, music tells the story of our lives.

Desert Island Discs

Early in 2024, I had the pleasure of being a guest on *Desert Island Discs*.[2] For those who don't know, this is a much-loved BBC programme on Radio 4 that has been on the air since 1942 and is currently presented by Lauren Laverne. Each week a guest is invited to imagine themselves as a castaway on a desert island. They choose eight musical tracks or recordings (from which excerpts are played), plus a book (in addition to the Bible and the complete works of Shakespeare) and a luxury item. Discussion around these choices provides the opportunity for a conversation and a look back over the guest's life. Like countless others, I'm sure, I have imagined myself on a desert island many times and swapped suggestions with friends and family about what musical choices we might make, and which one record we would save if the waves were about to wash the others out to sea. It was a genuine delight to be invited on to the programme.

Since then, quite a number of people have asked me what the experience was like and whether I found it easy to make my choices. I should say that Lauren Laverne and her production team are extremely skilled at what they do. They carry out their research before the interview and know just enough about you to ask pertinent questions that give shape to a story. Having listened to many episodes over the years, I am in awe of the way coherent and engaging programmes are carved out of a person's memories, reflections and musical choices.

Listening to my own episode later – in the car on my own – was a surreal experience. It was like a dash through my life in forty-five minutes. Memories came flooding back, especially through the music, reconnecting me with people, places and emotions, and bringing to the fore experiences that have shaped me profoundly. These memories and experiences are not necessarily things I think about very often, or intentionally call to mind. They are simply there, part of me and of who I am. It was not only moving but also fun to engage with my life through the music. And for the record, it was very difficult indeed limiting the choice to just eight tracks!

In the chapters that follow, my hope is that we may hear some of the melodies of the season as I focus on themes that are central to – or touch on the events of – Advent. I'll be looking for connections between these and my own life experiences, and I invite you as reader to tune in and look for your own particular connections so that your life story too may be illuminated. I will not avoid difficult topics; nor will I provide you with easy answers. Instead, I will probe and look to find meaning amid nuance and contradiction in places where there is complexity and when it is not always possible to find neat and tidy solutions. In an age when social media and the general tone of public debate seek to polarise and draw people to binary opposites, I'm interested in the rich and fertile areas in between, where there are shades and contours, where beauty and pain reside together and where we encounter God.

I wonder if it would be helpful, as you prepare to read this book, to have a go at creating your own *Desert Island Discs*? The choices you make are likely to help you better understand yourself and the things that are important to you. They will probably prompt memories of early childhood and moments you shared with a parent or sibling or friend. They may remind you of seminal moments in your life – perhaps relating to events during your school years, or when you first fell in love, or experiences you had while travelling, or times when you were struggling with ill health or bereavement. How you choose and what you choose may surprise you, but as you continue reading, I hope you will feel assured that nothing in your life has been wasted, and that every experience holds within it the possibility of transformation.

Note: At the end of each chapter, I will reflect on a piece of music chosen for its resonance to the chapter's theme. If you would like to, please make use of the links to the various tracks. You may find that they provide extra, possibly unexpected, dimensions to your Advent journey.

1

The Magnificat

Along with many others, I enjoy listening to Tom Holland and Dominic Sandbrook spar on their popular and informative podcast *The Rest Is History*. Indeed, they're both scholars of some note, and Holland's *Dominion: The making of the Western mind* has been hailed as a ground-breaking work.[1] Providing a broad historical sweep, from the Persian invasion of Greece in 480 BC to the ongoing migration crisis in Europe today, it seeks to demonstrate how Christian beliefs and values have infiltrated and shaped our culture to such an extent that we no longer even notice. Western society has taken Christian values on board and absorbed them; they have become the norm, forming the basis of an ethical framework even for atheists, who no longer realise that secular philosophies too have their roots in Christianity. You might say that Christianity has become a victim of its own success, in that many who are utterly shaped by Christian *principles* no longer feel any attachment to or need for the Christian *faith*. Like a fish that fails to consider the nature of the sea or river it occupies, Christianity has become the waters in which we unthinkingly swim.

Made in the image of God

Now, I can't possibly do justice to the full scope of Holland's remarkable book here, and at 624 pages long it isn't for the faint-hearted, but if you aren't up to the challenge of reading it, yet your appetite has been whetted, you'll find a number of enlightening interviews with the author on YouTube and elsewhere. In particular, I recommend episode 52 of the podcast series *The Rest Is Politics (Leading)*, in which Holland is the guest of presenters Rory Stewart and Alastair Campbell.[2]

To echo what I've said above, Holland's central premise is that Christianity is responsible for having shaped our thinking (in the West, at least) about the intrinsic value of each individual. What we now refer to as human rights (a largely secular concept) has its roots in the Christian message about the worth and dignity of each person; we are all – prince and pauper alike – made in the image of God. Along with this idea sits another: that Christianity is responsible for having brought the weak and the marginalised centre stage, impressing upon our collective conscience the need to protect and care for those who are poorest and most vulnerable.

If this is so, then surely the starting place, the cradle in which this revolution began, was the Magnificat:

And Mary said,

'My soul magnifies the Lord,
    and my spirit rejoices in God my Saviour,

2

for he has looked with favour on the lowliness of his
  servant.
  Surely, from now on all generations will call me
    blessed;
for the Mighty One has done great things for me,
  and holy is his name.
His mercy is for those who fear him
  from generation to generation.
He has shown strength with his arm;
  he has scattered the proud in the thoughts of their
    hearts.
He has brought down the powerful from their
    thrones,
  and lifted up the lowly;
he has filled the hungry with good things,
  and sent the rich away empty.
He has helped his servant Israel,
  in remembrance of his mercy,
according to the promise he made to our ancestors,
  to Abraham and to his descendants for ever.'
(Luke 1:46–55)

Good news for the powerless

The words are so familiar that we may not always recognise
what an extraordinary response this is by Mary to the
earth-shattering invitation to become the mother of the
Son of God. When King Herod heard about the birth
of Jesus, he feared a worldly rival, while Jesus' disciples
later hoped he had come to overturn the political rule

of the Romans. Only Mary – a young and simple village girl – understood instinctively that the kingdom of God, which the birth of her son would usher in, had nothing to do with gaining political power or worldly wealth and influence. Rather, it was good news for the downtrodden and powerless. The angel's message changed Mary's life, and it would be no exaggeration to say that her song changed the world.

Before we explore this further, let me acknowledge that Mary has often divided Christians. Even today, as Christopher Cocksworth writes, 'there remains a degree of incomprehension between those who feel that some pay too much attention to Mary and those who feel that some neglect her'.[3] In traditions where she is central, Mary has been celebrated as a paragon of virtue and purity, and held up as the idealised image of femininity and motherhood: Mary meek and mild, gentle and subservient, suffering silently, selfless and obedient to a fault. These images are neither wholly accurate nor have they been particularly helpful for women down the ages. The 'virgin mother' is an impossible role model for any woman to emulate. In the face of it, women will always fail and fall short. Furthermore, the qualities often given to Mary, and which have been associated especially with the feminine, can be used (or abused) to keep women in places of subjugation and suppression. In too many cultures and traditions women are already expected to be silent and obedient, modest and compliant. Giving these attributes theological or religious justification through the person of Mary is constraining and can be dangerous. Certainly, Mary has something to teach us about humility and obedience, but these are *human* virtues. They are for men as well as women and for the haughty and arrogant; not for keeping the lowly in their place.

'No Mary, no Jesus'

In any case, Mary is so much more than her stereotype. She plays a crucial part in the story of the incarnation. In short, 'No Mary, no Jesus'.[4] And if we care to listen, two thousand years on, her voice still cuts through with refreshing honesty, confidence and challenge. Countless artists and writers have tried to re-imagine Mary, to help us notice and learn from the woman who was courageous and audacious, who chose to say yes to God. There is one such example in Ely Cathedral, a statue of Mary by David Wynne, which dominates the Lady Chapel. It divides opinion – some love it, others hate it (there are plenty of comments to view online) – but whatever you think of it, it's difficult to ignore or pass by without pondering what you may previously have missed about Mary's person and example.[5]

In her exuberant 'yes', Mary demonstrates the way of true obedience, reminding us that God never forces or coerces us, but gently invites our participation in bringing about the divine will. Mary's 'yes' meant she willingly embraced all that would follow – the greatest of joys and the deepest of sorrows, for the two are closely intertwined. The shame of being a single mother; the embarrassment of Jesus' retort, 'Who is my mother?' (Matthew 12:48);

the harrowing pain of the crucifixion – none of these can be divorced from the delight the Christ child brought to Mary's life. It was joy, along with a deep and enduring love and a sense of purpose in fulfilling her vocation, that fashioned who Mary became. Her example bids us recognise how our joys and sorrows may also be bound together; how it is that we often feel hurt and pain in connection with the people we love, or in situations in which there is also much to treasure.

In response to the angel's message, Mary's spirited defiance found voice in the song she sang. Even if you know the Magnificat well, go back to earlier in this chapter and take a moment to reread this much-loved passage from Luke 1:46–55, slowly and deliberately, and you might perhaps be surprised once again by its radical message and the passion it exudes.

God's way will prevail

The glorious truth is that the Magnificat is music *of* the soul as well as music *for* the soul. Its melodies can permeate our lives if we but pause to catch their strains: God sees and blesses us, not in our greatness and successes, but in our humility and smallness, our hurt and anguish. God who is holy and other is also tenderly close. God is merciful, longs to defend us and deals with those who are proud and cause us pain.

Now, we enter tricky territory here, because it doesn't always seem as though God is defending the weak against the strong. Often the weak are crushed and the strong become the conquerors. But I wonder if the message is twofold. First, it is a clarion call for all of us to play our part in ensuring that the ways of righteousness and mercy hold sway in our lives and communities. Each of us must be an agent for justice wherever we see injustice at work. Second, it is a reminder that in the scheme of things God's way will prevail, even if we cannot be sure exactly when and how. Mary is saying that although pain and suffering exist for now, there will come a time when all this will pass. There are echoes here of Psalm 90 and a foreshadowing of the Revelation of St John. Addressing God, the psalmist sings, 'A thousand years in your sight are like yesterday when it is past, or like a watch in the night' (Psalm 90:4), and John joins in with assurance that God 'will wipe every tear from their eyes ... mourning and crying and pain will be no more, for the first things have passed away' (Revelation 21:4).

Holding on to these melodies, humming them over and over, requires trust. Yet we have the comfort of knowing that in God's sight those who feel unimportant and insignificant are raised up, and those who are on the margins are beckoned into the centre: God lifts up the lowly and brings down the powerful from their thrones. God's promise to our ancestors, to Abraham and his descendants for ever, remains God's promise to us today.

Connecting with my roots

This drawing of the edges into the centre, this raising up or honouring of the small and insignificant, has played a part in how I understand my own life story. In the spring of 2017, my family and I were living in Oakham, Rutland. My husband, Lee, was a parish priest and I was working part time for the Diocese of Peterborough. We had three young children still at home. Having been ordained some years earlier in 1998, I had often had a sense that my ministry required of me, in some way, to connect with my roots in the Persian Anglican Church, but I had no idea how or what that might involve. Having my first child in 2000, and the arrival later of twins, changed my life profoundly. I gave up stipendiary ministry for several years, before returning part time in 2010.

The call to explore episcopal ministry as Bishop of Loughborough in the Diocese of Leicester, came unexpectedly and was a huge surprise. From the first moment I felt an unavoidable contradiction. On one hand, nothing had prepared me for this: I didn't have the relevant experience and clearly they must have the wrong person. On the other hand, everything had prepared me for this: all my experiences had brought me to this place, and it was not so much about me and my achievements as about what I symbolised. I have lived in exile for over forty years, having left Iran at the age of thirteen in 1979, when the Islamic Revolution swept through the country, throwing our lives and that of the Church into disarray.[6] The Anglican community in Iran has always been small and vulnerable, and now it is so tiny as to be virtually insignificant in human terms. Yet it remains precious to me, and Mary's song assures me that it remains precious to and beloved by God. My appointment as a bishop in the

Church of England is perhaps in a strange way symbolic of that. For this dear community, marginal and lowly in the vastness of the Anglican Communion worldwide, has metaphorically been drawn into the centre through the appointment of a bishop in England.

That's why I often feel part of my calling is to remind people that God has not forgotten Christians who suffer persecution – in Iran, or in other places where the Church is fragile. Having become Bishop of Chelmsford in 2021, I find myself, extraordinarily, in the House of Bishops and the House of Lords – the quintessential centre of the establishment. But I try never to forget that I am there not through my own merits, but to represent something more profound, which is, in Mary's words, that the lowly find favour and are lifted up. And this realisation brings with it a sense of responsibility to use my voice, wherever I can, to promote the enduring melody at the heart of the Magnificat.

This is my story. Yours will be different, of course. What we can be sure of is that God works through the fabric of each and every life, weaving patterns that are unique and wonderful. To participate fully, we must be open to the unexpected, ready to notice new colours and contours, even if we can't yet make out the full picture. Indeed, we may need to wait for eternity for that. Until then, we strive to do our best to make sense of things; to connect the threads of our lives with those of others; to play our part, saying along with Mother Mary, 'Here am I, the servant of the Lord; let it be with me according to your word' (Luke 1:38); to sing with her, 'My soul magnifies the Lord, and my spirit rejoices in God my Saviour' (Luke 1:46–47).

Giovanni Battista Pergolesi: *Stabat Mater*

The piece of music I've chosen to accompany this chapter is, perhaps surprisingly, not a setting of the Magnificat. That's partly because I found I simply couldn't pick one from the myriad of compositions on offer – but I encourage anyone who wishes, to search them out and start listening. What I have selected instead is Pergolesi's *Stabat Mater,* in which the Mary we encounter is not so much the intrepid singer of a revolutionary song as the heart-broken mother witnessing the crucifixion of her son.

Giovanni Battista Pergolesi (1710–36) was an Italian composer of the baroque period and, despite his short life, fairly influential. The *Stabat Mater* was his final work, composed after he had fallen ill with tuberculosis, and completed shortly before his death at the age of twenty-six. It was written for two soloists and a string orchestra, and the words are taken from a thirteenth-century hymn to Mary. The Latin text portrays Mary's suffering as she stands at the foot of the cross, and the title translates as 'Sorrowful Mother'.

The hymn is deeply emotive and has been described as exploding with torment and lacerating grief. Pergolesi's music, through a series of evocative styles and techniques, serves to heighten the emotion. In the opening movement, for example, it is impossible to miss the weeping suspensions that repeatedly delay resolution and add to the intensity of the minor key. Somewhat controversially for the time, however, Pergolesi also used rhythms, syncopations and decorative trills that some have criticised as frivolous and out of place (he was also known for his works of comic opera).

I find the work achingly tender, and its beauty often leads me to tears. Pergolesi plumbs the depths of Mary's grief, even as he was surely contemplating the briefness of his own life and impending death, but he brings us at last to a final prayer of hope, which reminds us (as expressed in my introduction) that however deep the pain, there is always the possibility of transformation.

One of my favourite recordings of the *Stabat Mater* is conducted by Nathalie Stutzmann with the Orfeo 55 ensemble and soloists Philippe Jaroussky (countertenor) and Emöke Barath (soprano).[7]

For reflection

1 'In her exuberant "yes", Mary demonstrates the way of true obedience.' Has your understanding of Mary changed in any way through reading this chapter?
2 Reflecting on the melodies of the Magnificat listed in this chapter, which seems most relevant to you at the moment?
3 Can you think of an instance when you felt God was prompting you to act? Was there a tangible outcome you might share with others?

2

Flight

Migration has been with us since the dawn of time. It features in stories, myths and legends handed on from generation to generation, as well as in accounts of historical events. Think back to what you absorbed as a child. If you went to Sunday school, you're likely to be familiar with the cast of characters below. Migration is in the Bible right from the start.

Old Testament journeys

Early in the book of Genesis, Adam and Eve are expelled from the garden of Eden and must find a new home elsewhere (Genesis 3:24). Cain, their first-born son, murders his brother Abel and becomes 'a fugitive and a wanderer on the earth' (Genesis 4:12). Noah is instructed to build the ark before being sent on a voyage across the waters that have gathered on the face of the earth. Traditionally, he eventually arrives on Mount Ararat where he blesses his sons and tells them: 'Be fruitful and multiply, and fill the earth' (Genesis 9:1). Then in Genesis 12:1, Abram (later Abraham) is obedient to God's instruction: 'Go from your country and your kindred and your father's house to the land that I will show you.'

A few generations on, Joseph – memorably depicted in Tim Rice and Andrew Lloyd Webber's witty, poignant musical *Joseph and the Amazing Technicolor Dreamcoat* – is attacked by his brothers and subsequently sold by them into slavery in Egypt. There, after building a new life, he eventually brings his father, Jacob, and the entire household to reside with him (Genesis 37 – 50). But when the family grows in number to become the people of Israel, they once again find themselves on the move.

The books of Exodus, Leviticus, Numbers and Deuteronomy tell of the Israelites' departure from Egypt under Moses' guidance, and the forty years they spend wandering in the wilderness before Joshua finally leads them into the promised land. There follows a further period of exile when the armies of King Nebuchadnezzar lay siege to Jerusalem, forcibly deporting the children of Israel to Babylon (2 Kings 24).

As an Iranian, it is a huge delight to me that it was under the reign of Cyrus the Great of Persia that the Temple in Jerusalem was rebuilt, so that any Jews who chose to could return from Babylon and worship freely (Ezra 1:2–4). Arguably, King Cyrus gave birth to the notion of religious tolerance. He modelled a way for people of difference – whether displaced or rooted – to live alongside one another in peace. The Cyrus Cylinder, or Charter, sometimes called 'the first charter of human rights', stands as testament to this idea, and if you wish, you can go and see it on display in the British Museum in London.

We could continue with Hagar and Ishmael, the child Samuel, Ruth and Naomi, Jonah … the list is endless. In story after story the Bible introduces us to migrants, refugees and asylum seekers. Some have fled, others are forced to leave by circumstances, and still others go in search of better lives. But they are all united in being far from home; they are outsiders searching for a new identity and sense of belonging. And all hang on to the hope of transformation.

New Testament and contemporary migration

These stories of movement and flight spill over from the Hebrew Bible into the books of the New Testament, including the events that take place during Advent and Christmas. Before he was even born, Jesus' life began with a journey. A decree from the emperor Augustus required each person to be registered in the town they were from, and Joseph, whose family had clearly migrated over the years, had to comply (Luke 2:1–4). The account of the journey he and Mary made is retold each year during the season of Advent, and its familiarity may well numb us to how momentous it truly was. This young couple were expecting a baby in the days when giving birth was a much more risky and dangerous life event than it is now. They were frightened and uncertain, and the route they were travelling from Nazareth to Bethlehem in Judea was likely to have been treacherous. They were undoubtedly hoping and expecting to return home as soon as they could, though things turned out differently, as we know.

This enforced trip to Bethlehem meant that when Jesus was born, there was no loving family to welcome him; no friends or natural community around to offer wider support. Instead, his parents found themselves in a strange place, reliant on the goodwill and kindness of strangers. But how would the people among whom they found themselves respond to a request to make space for an unknown woman and her fiancé? They had come from God knows where … an unmarried woman expecting a child. They might have been scavengers, trying to sponge off the goodness of others, seeking to take shelter and resources that rightfully belonged to the locals …

The idea of giving birth in a stable (which is where the couple ended up) seems pretty bleak, and we tend to think of the inn-keeper as begrudging and lacking magnanimity. Yet modest and humble though this accommodation may have been, it was likely all he (or she?) had left, and the offer of shelter and relative warmth might be regarded as an act of some generosity.

While they were in Bethlehem, the Holy Family received word that King Herod, fearful of the influence of the Christ child, was intent on destroying him. So instead of returning home, they began another arduous journey, fleeing to Egypt for protection until it was safe to go back to Nazareth. Two millennia later, during the most recent conflict between Israel and Palestine, many Gazans found themselves doing exactly the same. With so many countries refusing to open their doors, those who were able sought, by any means they could, to find shelter and safety across the border in Egypt.

The fact is that anxious and despairing people far from home have always existed. We see them today in the guise of Ukrainians, Afghans, Syrians, Iranians, Iraqis,

Sudanese, Eritreans, Palestinians ... Reliant on the capacity of strangers for kindness, such souls may nonetheless bring untold gifts to their host communities. Just imagine what was in store for the unsuspecting inn-keeper once the shepherds, rapturously prompted by a chorus of angels, began arriving!

Whatever your view on the facts of the Advent and Christmas stories, they movingly convey that blessings come when we open our arms to those we do not know. The stories implore us to soften our hearts. They entreat us to pause and reflect, to remember that behind every statistic is an individual, a family, a child even, with their own joys and sorrows, hopes and dreams. The migrant and the refugee are people like you and me, and very little separates 'us' from 'them': only a handful of circumstances, an accident of birth, a twist of fate in the arena of international geo-politics.

Here is rich music for the soul.

Impossible choices

In March 2024, I was speaking at a debate in the House of Lords on the Rwanda Bill, which was then passing through parliament. The Bill (which has since been rescinded) was designed to send to Rwanda asylum seekers who had arrived in Britain on a small boat – without their claims first being heard and processed in the UK. I was concerned in particular about the potential impact of this on children, and I made the point that although the legislation was only intended for use with individuals over eighteen, evidence shows that age verification processes are notoriously unreliable. It is not unusual for a child to be assessed as older than they actually are. Given this is the case, who among us, I wondered, faced with a similar situation, would want to subject their own child or grandchild to such a process? I was challenged by another member, who wanted instead to know what kind of person would be prepared to endanger their child by putting them on a small boat in the first place.

Can you imagine how desperate someone would have to be to do such a thing? How unthinkably dreadful their circumstances? I replied that I certainly couldn't pass judgement on an unfortunate parent who was having to make an impossible choice between the lesser of two evils.

When my speaking time was up and I sat down, the image that flooded my mind was of a young woman from many centuries ago, Jochebed, the mother of Moses. Knowing that Pharaoh had ordered the killing of all male Hebrew babies, Jochebed, when she could no longer keep her son safe, placed him in a basket made of reeds and set him afloat on the waters (Exodus 2:3–4). She had no idea if they would be waters of life or waters of death, and who knows what agonies she went through, hoping against hope that someone would find the baby and offer him a safer, better life. Fortunately, someone did, and Moses grew up to lead God's people from slavery in Egypt towards freedom in the promised land.

These are not new themes; they are human stories as old as the hills.

A sense of belonging

The notion of welcome for the stranger is particularly pertinent to me, having arrived in the UK as a refugee from Iran in 1980. It has been my experience that good integration and finding a sense of belonging are based essentially on two things: the warmth of welcome and friendship experienced, and having the opportunity to contribute and find a sense of purpose. Since my schooldays, I have benefited hugely from the kindness and generosity of many: those who have given me opportunities; those who have believed in me when my own confidence has been low; those who have helped me, gradually and over time, to find my place and give back to the country that took my family in when we needed safety and protection.

We arrived well over forty years ago, when the world and the context we were living in were very different. There were fewer refugees, no dangerous boat crossings, and immigration generally wasn't such a hotly debated topic. There was racism, of course, and many immigrants have their own often harrowing stories to tell of that. But there was no official 'hostile environment', and public rhetoric was less toxic and divisive. As a family, we had our challenges and it took time to settle and find our way, but compared with many today, we had what I usually refer to as a soft landing.

Integration is not easy or straightforward. It requires intentionality, goodwill and a willingness to see things from the perspective of others. Our churches can play a key role in nurturing our God-given impulse to welcome, care for and love the stranger.

So, for many migrants, a sense of belonging can grow out of – and be nurtured by – a feeling of being welcomed and given an opportunity to contribute. I want now to touch on another related theme, which is that of identity. I'd like to explore what flight (the subject of this chapter) and the Advent season generally have to say to us at a time when many are looking to secure a stronger sense of identity, regardless of whether they have been physically displaced or not.

The loss of identity

You may already be familiar with the idea that to discover who we truly are, first we have to lose ourselves. This was surely Mary's experience: from the moment she heard the angel's message, nothing could ever be the same again. Mary lost her place within her community, her sense of who she was and her expectations of what her life would be like. She then had to begin the process of discovering her new self, the one that God was calling her to become, with all the joy and sorrow that would entail. Nothing is wasted, of course, so her old self will have informed the person she was growing into. Nonetheless, there is no escaping the fact that sometimes you have to lose your identity to find it.

This is true not only for those who suffer displacement as refugees and asylum seekers, but also for those who experience serious illness, divorce, grief, abuse ... in fact, profound loss or injustice of any kind. Such suffering can strip us of who we thought we were; the old assurances and securities disappear, and the world begins to look very different.

At times like these, either we can remain stuck or we can begin the climb to a new sense of self, which may be slow and painful but also possibly transformative. This subject has long fascinated novelists, and there are many books that play with the theme of identity and losing yourself to find yourself. One of my favourites is William Boyd's *Ordinary Thunderstorms*.[1] It's a book I read many years ago and it made a vivid impression on me, first because it's a great novel by a great author, and second because I happened to come across it shortly after having a really bizarre experience at work …

I was involved in a project at Northampton University. Returning after the summer break, I discovered that, due to some mishap, I had been deleted from the computer system. Apparently, one contract had come to an end and another should have begun a few days later, but instead the system had eliminated me altogether. The computer would not recognise my password. I had no email address. I was not on the list of staff. To all intents and purposes I did not exist. As such, I discovered I could do no work. I couldn't access my diary or my contacts, my emails or my files. I spent the whole of my first day trying to persuade various departments that I was who I said I was and imploring them to please give me back my identity.

In *Ordinary Thunderstorms*, something along these lines happens to the young climatologist Adam Kindred.

At the beginning of the book, we encounter Adam as he faces a terrible choice, requiring a split-second decision, the implications of which prove to be monumental and change the course of his life for ever. If he is to avoid being destroyed, Adam must go underground and disappear completely. Only by giving up his identity can he save himself in the moment, and the rest of the book is about how he begins the process of discovering who he is now becoming. To use a religious metaphor, he has to die in order to rise again.

A sense of worth

We probably seldom stop to think about what it means to have an identity, and I don't want to submerge us in deep philosophical waters here, but let's at least ponder the following: what gives you your sense of worth and makes you feel real? Is it your work? Your relationships? Your place of birth? Or even your name?

When I arrived in England I considered changing my name to something that would make my life easier – something I wasn't required to spell out all the time or forced to hear endlessly mispronounced. Yet, though this seemed a logical step, I couldn't bring myself to take it. Even as a teenager I sensed it would be a betrayal of my identity.

Perhaps your identity is more tied up with formal documents: your birth certificate, passport, bank account, credit cards – the things that confirm who you are in black and white and allow strangers to recognise you as you. Let me ask you to consider a few questions (I have no easy answers myself): if these things were taken away and you had no name or documents, would you lose your identity? If you lost your job and those close to you, would you stop being you? If you went through unspeakable suffering and had no place of belonging, would you cease to exist?

Some people may feel that such a profound loss would be the result of circumstances like these. However, in his book *Extraordinary Awakenings: From trauma to transformation*,[2] psychologist Steve Taylor explores how it is that for some people intense psychological trauma – bereavement, depression, imprisonment, military combat and so on – can lead to apparently miraculous and positive spiritual experiences. Through a combination of real-life stories and research, Taylor has discovered that this transformation relates to the *dissolution* of identity; it is as if intense suffering and stress somehow allow for the emergence of a deeper essential spiritual self. The threat of losing something we consider absolutely vital may, in fact, lead us to new depths beyond our imagining.

Perhaps that's why some of the ascetics and mystics of days gone by – Simeon Stylites and Teresa of Ávila, to name but two – actively sought their own suffering through self-denial or self-inflicted pain as the path towards spiritual awakening. In our modern understanding, such extremes are not to be recommended. Yet throughout religious history, the practice of meditation or contemplative prayer (on which more later) has required an overcoming of the ego in order to discover something new and experience the divine. At such times, we may find ourselves hearteningly aware of the *cantus firmus*, the deepest melody of the music of the soul.

Mahan Mirarab: 'Say Your Most Beautiful Word'

The music of Mahan Mirarab, an Iranian singer–song writer who now lives and works in Austria, fits well with the theme of this chapter. Both he and his wife, the singer Golnar Shahyar with whom he often performs, had to leave the familiarity of their homeland to find the freedom to develop as musicians.

Mirarab has cultivated a style that draws on traditional Persian music enriched by influences from many other cultures and musical genres, including jazz, Afro-Caribbean rhythms, Western classical, and pop music. He plays a guitar that has two separate fingerboards, one of which is fretless, allowing him to blend and improvise, moving between Eastern and Western soundscapes.

In a track called 'Say Your Most Beautiful Word', Mirarab sets to music a poem of the same title, composed by the famous twentieth-century Iranian poet, writer and journalist Ahmad Shamloo (1925–2000). Shamloo was politically active throughout his life, a social critic both during the Shah's time and after the Islamic Revolution, and often found himself on the wrong side of the authorities. He was imprisoned twice.

Mirarab's music, Shahyar's voice and the words of Shamloo come together in 'Say Your Most Beautiful Word' to great effect. The piece is a potent reminder that it is possible to resist bitterness and hate in the face of injustice and suffering, even though these may have taken you far from home, placed you among strangers and forced you to rediscover who you are. Finding and repeating, again and again, the 'most beautiful word' is a powerful response in the face of all kinds of human agony. Neither music nor love is futile or fruitless but can instead transform pain in a creative act of resistance.[3]

For reflection

1 Can you think of a time when you were desperate for help? Perhaps you'd lost your wallet or travel pass, or had an accident. What happened?
2 'The migrant and the refugee are people like you and me, and very little separates "us" from "them".' How do you find yourself responding to this statement?
3 On a day-to-day basis, how strong is your sense of identity? Have there been times when you've felt you have lost sight of who you are? Do you feel able to reflect on or share something of the circumstances?

3

Violence

We have been exploring circumstances and experiences through which we may become better attuned to the music of the soul and reach a deeper understanding of God's loving presence in our world. And it will have become clear that however delightful it may be to imagine that Advent and Christmas are mainly about angels and stars, nativity plays and twinkling lights, this is simply not the case. For there is violence lurking in these stories and accounts; they are littered with moments of brutality.

Looking reality in the eye

It is not easy to dwell on the dark side of humanity, but Advent invites us to abide, to stay awhile, to grapple with the grittiness of life. In any case, it's never a good idea to ignore reality, however hard; much better to look it straight in the eye. That's what we'll be doing in this chapter, and my hope is that we will end it reassured that hatred and pain need not destroy us nor have the final word.

The events of Advent and Christmas are inextricably bound up with the events of Holy Week and Good Friday. Each year, it is the Feast of Christ the King (the last Sunday of the church calendar) which propels us into this new season. And in celebrating Christ as King, it is impossible to overlook the place of the cross, and the truth that Jesus' kingship was demonstrated through the shame and violence of crucifixion. John the Baptist, as the one who prepared the way for Jesus' ministry, is remembered on not one but two Sundays during Advent. His story is also infused with tragedy: Herod, at the behest of his wife and daughter, ordered the imprisoned John's beheading (Mark 6:14–29).

There are two days given over to commemorating the martyrdom of St Stephen (on 26 December) and St Thomas of Canterbury (on 29 December). As if those two commemorations weren't poignant enough, cradled between them on 28 December is the Massacre of the Innocents (which we touched on earlier), surely the most repugnant of all. This event, outlined in Matthew's Gospel and right at the heart of the Christmas story, tells of Herod ordering the execution of all male children under the age of two in the region of Bethlehem (Matthew 2:1–18). The angels may have declared that the baby born in a manger brought a message of peace and goodwill to all, but to the emperor Jesus represented a grave threat.

Years later, in the days before his death, Jesus would again cast fear into the hearts of some of the powerful, when he rode on a donkey into Jerusalem and was greeted rapturously by the crowds. Ordered to stop the people from chanting, his chilling response echoes across the centuries and rings a warning bell to all who seek, fearfully and forcibly, to maintain control today: 'I tell you, if these [people] were silent, the very stones would shout out' (Luke 19:40). Sometime after that, when Stephen faced the crowds, challenging long-held religious assumptions through his extraordinary preaching, it was likely a mixture of fear and anger that drove the people to pick up and throw the stones that killed him. Likewise, in twelfth-century England it was fear of Thomas Becket's influence that led King Henry II to call for his permanent removal.

Today too, in many countries across the globe, despotic regimes govern through violence, destroying anything they perceive as a threat to their survival. Countless numbers experience persecution – arrest, unjust captivity, torture or even execution. Yet remarkably, courageous and peaceful protests continue, bubbling to the surface from time to time, as those who may feel they have nothing to lose allow themselves to keep hoping for justice and liberty.

The Iranian Revolution

My own life, in which I have experienced so much grace and blessing, has also been touched by violence. I have written more fully about this elsewhere,[1] but for now let me simply say that the Islamic Revolution of 1979, which turned Iran upside down, had an immense impact on our small Anglican community.

My father, a convert from Islam, was the first indigenous Persian bishop of the Anglican Church in Iran. During the initial eighteen months or so of the revolution, a raft of injustices was perpetrated against our Christian community, including the confiscation of several institutions, raids on properties, the harassment of members and the murder of one of our clergy, Arastoo

Sayyah, in his home in the city of Shiraz. My father was briefly imprisoned and later survived an attempt on his life in which my mother was shot and injured. For my family, the culmination of these horrors was the assassination of my brother, Bahram, aged twenty-four, in May 1980. He became a scapegoat for our father, who was the real target but abroad at the time. A young man – with so much potential and a desire to serve his country – was gunned down in the prime of life because the small church community, made up primarily of converts and second- or third-generation Christians, was seen as a threat to the emerging Islamic Republic.[2] It was a tragically bleak reminder that power warped by fear and hatred makes for a dangerous cocktail and none of us is immune from its effects.

Today, Bahram is among those remembered in the Book of Modern Day Martyrs in Canterbury Cathedral's Corona Chapel. His story (along with Arastoo's and others') intertwines with that of Thomas Becket from eight centuries earlier, pointing to the uncomfortable reality that persecution and martyrdom are not things of the past; they are not ancient phenomena that ended with the legalising of Christianity under Constantine in the fourth century. Rather, in following the example of Christ, the Church and individual Christians should always expect to experience suffering if they are truly living out their calling: the message of Christianity, from the Magnificat, through Advent, the incarnation and beyond, turns on its head the values of the world, so can threaten and induce fear in the hearts of the powerful. It is no surprise then that martyrdom, which is as old as the stoning of Stephen, is also as contemporary as the kidnap, torture and killing of twenty-one Christian men by ISIS in 2015 and the beheading of Father Jacques Hamel, the French Roman Catholic priest killed in 2016 by Islamic extremists.

Suffering

Suffering as a part of faith is a theme spelled out eloquently in both the Old and the New Testament and I'd like to look at two examples: the first from the life of Job and the second from the writings of the apostle Peter.

The book of Job begins with these reassuring words: 'There was once a man in the land of Uz whose name was Job. That man was blameless and upright, one who feared God and turned away from evil' (Job 1:1). Yet despite this promising start, over the course of the ensuing forty-two chapters appalling misfortunes and violent calamities befall Job, nearly crushing him in the process. In chapter 30 he cries out to God,

> Did I not weep for those whose day was hard?
> > Was not my soul grieved for the poor?
> But when I looked for good, evil came;
> > and when I waited for light, darkness came.
> My inward parts are in turmoil, and are never still;
> > days of affliction come to meet me.
> (Job 30:25–27)

Job has been the subject of many studies and reflections on the problem of evil and why it is that good people suffer.

But despite the wisdom and insight of some of the greatest minds, we are not that much closer to providing answers for those who find themselves in anguish. It is a painful truth that none of us is exempt from suffering, and faith does not protect us or provide immunity.

In the New Testament, writing to persecuted Christian communities in Asia Minor, the apostle Peter says: 'Beloved, do not be surprised at the fiery ordeal that is taking place among you to test you, as though something strange were happening to you. But rejoice in so far as you are sharing Christ's sufferings' (1 Peter 4:12–13).

For most of us, it is easy to forget – because we live in relative safety – that there is nothing wishy washy about the Christian faith. The invitation to follow Christ demands a response from each of us and that response, if lived out fully, can be costly. For some it leads to martyrdom. And suffering, including when it involves violent force and injustice, is present in the Christian story from the events of Advent onwards.

Suffering comes in many guises and can often feel like a violent assault, emotionally and psychologically if not literally. We encounter it in times of serious illness, the grief of losing a loved one or coming to terms with the breakdown of a relationship. It can catch us unawares in our own vulnerability – those times, for example, when we fail, fall short or make a mistake that leads to unintended and damaging consequences. Suffering is not partial to wealth or poverty, to class or skin colour, and it is no respecter of time and season. People suffer and violence occurs during Advent and Christmas just as much as any other time of the year.

However, pain and suffering are never to be glorified, excused or justified. We may have no easy answers, but that doesn't mean we don't care about its effects. In situations of injustice, it is our responsibility to speak and act for change wherever possible. While still in Iran and later in exile, my father never stopped calling out the atrocities committed against the Church in the country he loved, demanding justice for the Christian community. It did not change things materially – institutions and properties have not been returned, others too have been imprisoned, no one has been held accountable for the murders – but my father's cry for justice continued until the day he died, resounding with a fierce honesty and a desire to make sure that no one would ever forget.

Judgement

If violence and pain are Advent themes, so too is judgement: another difficult concept we often dance around. God's judgement – the conviction that all people will be judged according to their actions and beliefs – is an important Christian precept whose potency has been somewhat diluted in recent times, as characteristics like God's love and forgiveness have come to the fore. But make no mistake, our hope and expectation for the coming of God's kingdom is also an anticipation of God's coming judgement, and we do well to be mindful of that. The word, or the concept it encapsulates, is sometimes used loosely and even dangerously by those Christians who take for themselves the role that rightly belongs to God. Too many pass judgement on others, including fellow Christians, making themselves the arbiters of truth. There are times, in a court of law, for example, or when serious harm is being done, when a judge or someone with authority must pass judgement and decide a sentence. But as a rule, and certainly on matters of faith, we should be very wary indeed of ever taking it upon ourselves to judge the eternal fate of our fellow human beings. Untold psychological and emotional harm can be done, especially by those in positions of influence, wounding people who are already fragile and vulnerable. Instead, each of us might do better reminding ourselves that we too will one day be judged, and may God have mercy upon our souls. We can debate and disagree on matters of doctrine and faith, and there will always be differences of perspective, but all of us, the powerful and the powerless, are together walking the path towards the judgement seat of God. And we can be sure that those who have brought violence on others, will also have to account for their actions, and God's judgement will fall heavy upon them.

We have reflected a little on the bigger picture and issues relating to nations, systems and organisations, recognising the need for justice and the coming judgement of God. But what about the smaller canvas of our own lives and communities – those times when individuals experience severe pain, sometimes unjustly and violently? Some of the same principles apply but again, there are no easy answers to finding the way towards healing and wholeness. Sometimes the best we can do is stay with others in their suffering, remaining alongside them rather than fleeing in embarrassment or impatience, allowing them to weep or cry out in distress and anger. Sometimes the best we can do is bear our own pain with as much grace as we can muster, acknowledging our vulnerability, while trying to hang on to those things that are precious and wonderful.

Forgiveness

The response to suffering, especially that which is caused by another, is sometimes presented as two polarised options. You either cling on to the hurt and anger, determined never to let go; or you forgive, forget and move on. In truth, there is a vast expanse in between, full of nuance and contradictions. The journey from woundedness to wholeness is never linear, it looks different for each person, there are no right and wrongs, and we may never fully arrive. But at its heart, I wonder if it involves the following: the desire to move forward well and an openness towards the possibility of forgiveness and transformation, courage to get through the hard days, willingness to seek help when necessary, the ability to put yourself in the shoes of others and the capacity to notice the blessings and beauty of life. It was, I believe, Hannah Arendt, a twentieth-century German historian and philosopher, who explored the possibility that the virtue of forgiveness might lie in the fact that it provides a route out of apparently irreversible situations. This is not to be confused with the idea that injustices should be suffered in silence; for we should always be those who speak and act against injustice wherever we see it. Rather, it suggests a way of living that is orientated away from self-interest and towards the needs of others.[3]

Grace

I was listening recently to an interview with the author, Sarah Perry, about her latest novel, *Enlightenment*, which explores science and religion through the lenses of astronomy and reformed theology.[4] She spoke eloquently and beautifully both about suffering and about the idea of grace. She made a fascinating association between suffering and the Laws of Kepler.

Johannes Kepler was a German astronomer and mathematician who in the seventeenth century defined three laws that keep bodies in orbit in motion; perpetually going round and round. 'When considering suffering, you can tell people that their heartbreak or fear will pass,' Perry said. 'It will. But it will return, because that is part of the human condition.' Kepler's theory of the orbit leads to what she called 'the brutal wisdom that things pass and then return'. While acknowledging that injustice and suffering are not how things are meant to be, at some level we also have to accept that hurt and pain are part of being human and in that sense will always be with us. Having accepted these two principles, we then seek to navigate our way as best we can between the two – acceptance of suffering on the one hand, and resistance against pain and injustice on the other. What helps us do that, I was reminded by Perry, is the idea of grace which she described as 'an un-earned gift – a moment that arrives out of the universe that you didn't earn, you didn't deserve, and you didn't ask for'. Moments of grace appear and we can choose either not to notice them or to meet them with gratitude and joy. 'The most ordinary day,' Perry said, 'is a catalogue of acts of grace, if you're alert to them'. This alertness instils a sense of gratitude and it carries through to a graciousness towards others.[5]

During Advent and Christmas, I remember perhaps more vividly than at any other time of year the happy, carefree and joy-filled days of my childhood in Iran, as well as the darker times when we were engulfed by violent events outside of our control. Deep thankfulness for all that is good mingles with feelings of loss and the pain of rupture from home and country. Somewhere in the mix of gratitude and sorrow, there is the possibility of transformation. The remembrance of those we have lost and the pain of the burdens we carry are met by the joy of the coming of the Christ child who brings hope and the prospect of new beginnings.

'Bahram's Melody'

My brother Bahram had a great zest for living. He was clever and funny, loyal and loving; serious in his intentions but with a mischievous streak, always looking for the humour in things. Bahram lives on in so many ways – through his friends, through our memories and through some of his personal traits that I now see in my children. He brought so much joy and touched our lives in profound ways, leaving a very great impression through his relatively short time with us.

Among other things, Bahram was a fine pianist and musician. Every five years since his death, a memorial concert has been held in the chapel of his old college at Oxford, Jesus, where he was an undergraduate in the 1970s. Friends and family join with current members of the college to remember Bahram with thanksgiving and to celebrate his short but extraordinary life through music. Several of his contemporaries from Oxford attend these events faithfully, and with the passing of each five years we see how Bahram, frozen in our minds as a young man of twenty-four, would have aged. These are poignant occasions yet always with an undercurrent of joy. At the ninth such concert, held just days ago as I write this, I was struck especially by the profound sense of hope and an awareness of new life through the exuberant performances of the young musicians. The Lord gives and the Lord takes away.

A few years before he died, Bahram composed a hymn tune for words written by my father. My father was a poet and many of his hymns remain as part of the Persian hymnal, which is still used in Iran and across the world by many Iranians. The words were translated by Norman Sharp, and although they don't quite capture the poetry of the Persian, they do enable the hymn to be sung in English too:

Violence

You, O my God, gifts of knowledge give to me,
that hidden mysteries I may clearly see.
Free me from inward fights, life's tangled skein.
My torn heart heal, O Lord, make me glad again.

Spirit of God, source of wisdom, guidance, life,
yet to receive these gifts, we must daily die.
Spirit of Jesus Christ reaches our pain,
consciences weak through guilt, he makes whole again.

Love from the human heart through selfishness will
    fail,
love that your Spirit gives, causes it to pale.
Lord, fill us deep within, so friends will know,
even to enemies, your love we can show.

Jesus, we'll follow you, servant hearts we need,
with your compassion, Lord, others we will feed.
Grant us to follow you, never retreat,
gladly to wash and cleanse one another's feet.

People without God are living for themselves,
bringing such sep'rateness, suffering and fear.
Come, Lord, and show us all your power to heal,
uproot the source of hate, may your peace reign here.

You, O my God, gifts of knowledge give to me,
that hidden mysteries I may clearly see.
Living obediently, grace you'll endue,
my soul and character you'll make wholly new.

In 1985, the hymn tune was arranged for the first memorial concert as a quartet for flute, violin, cello and piano by my then music teacher, David Peacock. It has been performed many times since. The piece is now affectionately known as 'Variations on Bahram's Melody'. It was one of my choices on *Desert Island Discs*, played by my eldest son, Gabriel, who is a cellist, and three of his musician friends. It is a haunting melody, beautifully arranged, but more importantly it is a reminder of all that was good about Bahram. It is music for the soul, playing on long after violence did its worst and Bahram was taken from us. In life and faith, some things can never be destroyed and there we find the possibility of healing and transformation.[6]

For reflection

1 When did you first become aware of the grittiness of life? Were there particular events or news stories that had an impact on you when you were still quite young?

2 Have you ever found yourself actively participating in an effort to bring about change? What were the circumstances?

3 Music can help us process feelings we may find difficult to acknowledge or express. Are there particular pieces that have helped you make sense of (or come more to terms with) suffering you've experienced?

4

Angels

When our children were small, one of their favourite Christmas books was a picture book called *Gabriel's Feather*.[1] The author, Elizabeth Laird, lived nearby and she and her husband had become good friends of ours. *Gabriel's Feather* is an enchanting retelling of the nativity story, beautifully illustrated by Bettina Paterson. It begins with the annunciation, but before Gabriel departs from Mary, a golden feather falls from his wings. This is picked up by a little bird, who transports it through the whole tale until, at the end, it is presented as a gift to the baby Jesus. Part of the charm of the book is looking for the feather hidden somewhere on each page.

Encountering angels

For both young and old, angels can be a subject of fascination. These days, the fall in the number of those attending church suggests that organised religion has ever less appeal. Many nonetheless long for something that is both bigger and beyond themselves; they want, at some level, to connect with the supernatural. Angels are one component of this form of popular religion, if we can call it that, and over the years I have read many articles on the subject. I have also heard first hand from people who have wanted to tell me about their experience of seeing an angel or angels – including some vivid and dramatic encounters. I haven't always known what to make of this. By nature, I confess, I'm a little sceptical; then again, it's always good to pause and wonder.

Certainly, the events of Advent and Christmas are littered with stories of angels, and several of the characters we meet during this season are visited by heavenly beings. There's Mary, of course, to whom the angel Gabriel comes with news of Jesus' birth. Then there's the priest Zechariah, married to Mary's cousin, Elizabeth. An angel appears to Zechariah to announce that he and his wife are to have a baby boy, John, who will prepare the way for the coming of the Lord. Zechariah is incredulous and asks for proof, since he and his wife are getting on in years, and for this lack of faith he is struck mute until after the boy is born. Joseph meets an angel several times in his dreams – first, convincing him to marry Mary even though she is already pregnant; later (as we have seen), telling him to take Mary and Jesus to safety in Egypt, to escape the wrath of King Herod; later still, prompting him to return to Israel once the threat of danger is over. The wise men are also warned in a dream to avoid Herod when returning to their own country, though there is no mention of angels specifically. But perhaps most spectacular of all is the story of the shepherds in Luke 2:8–14. An angel appears, bringing good news of the birth of the Saviour, before the skies are filled with 'a multitude of the heavenly host, praising God and saying, "Glory to God in the highest heaven, and on earth peace among those whom he favours!"' (vv. 13–14).

On each of these occasions, an angel or angels appear to indicate the presence of God. So, sceptic or not, perhaps it is worth spending a little time exploring what angels might mean, both in the Bible and for us today. First, a brief history to set the context.

A Christian understanding

Christians inherited their understanding of angels from the Jewish tradition, which was influenced by Egyptian culture, probably when the people of Israel were captive in the land of Egypt. From the earliest stages, angels were creatures for good, spirits of love and envoys bringing news. Later came the identification of individual angelic messengers: Gabriel, Michael, Raphael and Lucifer, the fallen angel or the devil. Then, in the space of little more than two centuries (from the third to the fifth), angels began taking on definite characteristics both in theology and in art. By the late fourth century, the Church had agreed that there were various categories of angels, each with their own appropriate focus and activities. There remained, however, a degree of disagreement about the *nature* of angels. Some argued that angels had physical bodies; others maintained they were entirely spiritual. Some thought they were divine creatures; others posited that they were between divine and human, immaterial beings of a sort, subordinate to God but above humanity.

Scripture in both the Old and the New Testament includes a good number of interactions between angels and humans, populating much loved biblical stories and punctuating significant points in the Christian calendar. In the Old Testament, it seems there is hardly a prophet, leader or character playing a significant part in the story of God's people who doesn't encounter an angel at some point. (Consider, for example, Abraham, Moses, Jacob, Hagar, the unnamed mother of Samson, Ezekiel and Isaiah.) In the New Testament, angels test Jesus in the wilderness; during Holy Week they comfort him in his hours of agony in the garden of Gethsemane; on Easter Day they announce his resurrection to the women who visit the empty tomb. In the book of Revelation, you can barely turn a page without meeting an angel or a cherub or a seraph. And this is really just scratching the surface. There's a whole lot more about angels in the Bible.

So, what is their purpose? How are we meant to understand them and interpret the part they play? The Christian concept is that they are messengers of God. They bring good news, as they did to Mary, Zechariah and the shepherds. They bring comfort and reassurance, as they did to Joseph when he was doubting himself and wondering if he should proceed with marriage to his betrothed. They bring words of caution, as they did when they warned Joseph of the danger posed by Herod and guided the wise men to return home via a different route. They also bring words of reproach and challenge, and their message is not always comfortable or welcome: Zechariah was admonished when he began to question God's purposes, and it's not beyond credibility that Joseph might actually have preferred to take the easier option of deserting Mary.

Pointing to a sign

However, more than being messengers, angels are also a sign or, perhaps more accurately, they point to a sign that God is at work in the world, often in unexpected ways. Angels draw our attention to things we may not immediately notice. For example, I suspect Luke was only too aware that the shepherds on the hillside best sum up what is, in fact, the scandal of Christmas. In first-century Palestine, shepherds were among the lowest on the social ladder – dirty, possibly smelly, itinerant workers. In contemporary terms, we might think along the lines of a group of Middle Eastern or East European immigrants, waiting on a street corner to see if they're going to be picked up that day for casual agricultural labour; or a homeless man living in a tent under a bridge; or a single mum trying to survive on a zero hours contract and Universal Credit. The truth of the matter, uncomfortable though it may be, is that it was to this sort of person – to those we might call *them* – rather than to *us*, that the message was given about the birth of the Messiah. We should never forget this extraordinary sign, this radical reversal of expectation, once again drawing into the centre that which is considered marginal. There are echoes here of the Magnificat and the music of Mary's song.

Every element of the Advent stories, every aspect of the stable scene, every joyful Christmas sound, celebrates and points towards one central truth – that God has become human for us, born as a little, gurgling scrap of humanity, a vulnerable babe wrapped in bands of cloth, but God nonetheless, Very God of Very God. This is a huge claim – one that many discount, some misunderstand and a few ridicule – but for Christians it is our joy and privilege to proclaim it. God has become human for us. And, crucially, that has implications for how we live our lives, because the message of the angels and the sign it points to simply turns the world upside down. So, if it is true (and I say 'if', not because I have any doubt personally but because it remains for each person to decide for themselves) – if it is true, then it should affect us deeply. We will each need, with the shepherds, to see the sign and recognise it for what it is; we will each need to gaze at the child and recognise him for who he is: none other than God in human form.

The glory of God

This message, this sign, is such that the angels could do none other than burst into joyful song in response. 'Glory to God in the highest heaven,' they sang as they visited the shepherds on that first Christmas night. Words repeated in word and song every Advent, every Christmas. But what does 'glory' actually mean and how might it be given to God in heaven?

The Hebrew word for glory used in much of the Old Testament has the simple meaning of heaviness, weight or value, and in everyday speech expressed the worth of a person, often in material terms. For example, in the Old Testament stories, Jacob's glory was his animals and servants, Joseph's his position in Egypt and King David's his authority over the people. But used of God, it came to have a greater significance, expressing something of divine splendour, power and majesty. And that is how the angels used it over the hills in Bethlehem, that those who heard it might recognise and pay homage to God's greatness.

And yet ... at the time of writing, war is raging in Europe following the Russian invasion of Ukraine; Gaza and Lebanon are in the grip of the most horrific battle that further threatens the fragile peace of the wider Middle East; and civil unrest and conflict are causing suffering and the mass movement of refugees in many parts of the world. In Britain, millions are homeless or in unsuitable accommodation and many are anxious about how to feed their children or heat their homes as the cost of living continues to rise.

How can we possibly sing of God's glory and greatness when our world is engulfed by so much violence and brokenness? It is a reasonable question to ask, and once again there are no easy answers. Yet there are choices we can make. We can choose to dwell awhile; to listen and try to catch the strain of the angels' song. Yes, there is painful dissonance, but there is also the possibility of reaching into difficult spaces – embracing perplexity – and opening ourselves to the presence of elusive and conflicting realities.

If we acknowledge for a moment God's glory – God's majesty, might, splendour and power – the natural question that then arises is: how is it that God demonstrates that glory and greatness? In particular, how is it that we witness and celebrate God's glory each and every Christmas, no matter what our circumstances or what is going on around us?

Well, you already know the answer. We witness and celebrate through the birth of a tiny baby, born in a dirty and smelly stable, to an unmarried young woman far from home. A baby who shows us that the essence of God's glory is *love*, a vulnerable love that will remain steadfast and true through the darkest of days, even to death on a cross.

It's worth repeating! God's glory, God's greatness and splendour, is simply and truly this: *God's love.*

And this love is shown in the ordinary things of life, even in the messiest and toughest of circumstances. This love overcomes all things and can never be quenched. This love lasts beyond death and never gives up on the possibility of new beginnings. No matter what our present reality, the song of the angels is one of hope for a better future. And we proclaim that hope in our words, by sharing the good news of Jesus Christ, and through our actions in seeking to build a better future in this life, even as we wait for the fulfilment of God's promise in the assurance of life after death. In countless ways, both personal and public, the angels' song reflects and proclaims God's glory, which is God's love.

A personal response

So why, despite all this, are many of us still a little uncomfortable with talk of angels, seeing them perhaps as a repository of all our unsolved spiritual projections? It is one thing to speak of the song they sang, quite another to reflect on the angelic beings themselves. Let me be clear: I do not know what angels are, what they look like or whether they really are to be found flying around the place as some people today would still have us believe. But I do know that I have met angels. Indeed, as I reflect on my life, I believe I have encountered many angelic messengers over the years, signifying God's presence and God's love.

I have been aware of angels attending people as they approach death. In particular, I recall the final days of my mother's life in the autumn of 2016. She had moved in with us three months earlier and we did our best to care for her; every day, various friends and family members would visit as she moved slowly towards the end. Finally, as her last breath came, I have no doubt that angels were present in the room in the form of each one of those waiting by the bedside, lovingly and patiently, transforming the pain of ending and loss.

I have glimpsed angels in the kindness people show one another. I am reminded frequently of the throwaway remark in the apostle Paul's letter to the Hebrews: 'Do not neglect to show hospitality to strangers, for by doing that some have entertained angels without knowing it' (Hebrews 13:2). As I visit different places around the Diocese of Chelmsford, and sometimes more widely, I meet individuals and groups who provide meals and overnight accommodation for people who have no homes; who extend support and friendship to asylum seekers and those who are lonely or bereaved; who offer free holiday meals and Christmas gifts to children who might otherwise go without. And when watching the news, I often notice angels hovering at the scene of a tragic accident or terrorist attack, bravely coming to the aid of those in danger or difficulty, without any thought for themselves or their safety.

I have met angels who have been bringing a message from God to a community. Many times, I have been part of a church, a place of work or an established team of some kind into which a newcomer has arrived with the eyes and ears of an outsider. If we have been ready and willing to receive it, such newcomers have been angels who have encouraged, challenged and helped us reassess ourselves and our priorities.

The more I reflect and allow my heart and mind to tune in to the mysterious ways of God, the more I imagine angels all around, waiting, loitering almost. This very day, you and I will have an opportunity to entertain an angel in one guise or another. I wonder if we'll notice.

As we embrace the darkness of Advent and wait in hopeful anticipation for all our longings to be fulfilled, let us seek to be angelically present to others, a sign of God's loving presence even in the midst of suffering, pain and confusion. All churches and Christian communities should be places where we are angels to one another and to those in our neighbourhood. When we are weary, we need angels to enliven us and allow us time to rest. When we are harsh, we need angels to soothe and love us. When we lack generosity, we need angels to model ways of warmth and openness. When there is confusion or uncertainty, we need the wisdom of angels to help us discern the way ahead. Where there is pain and hurt, we need angels to offer consolation and comfort.

I know deep in my being that the promises of God are true and that in recognising who Jesus is and what he did through his birth, death and resurrection, we see great and wonderful things. The power of the cross of Christ turns death to life, hatred to love and violence to gentleness, and it fans the flame of Advent hope. Why on earth, then, should I doubt the existence of angels? For surely they are daily ascending and descending between heaven and earth among those whose lives reflect God's love. We only need to open our eyes to see.

Nick Cave and the Bad Seeds: 'Into My Arms'

I came late to the music of the Australian singer and songwriter Nick Cave. To my shame, I had not even heard of him until I stumbled across the book *Faith, Hope and Carnage*, based on forty hours of intimate conversations between Nick Cave and the journalist Sean O'Hagan.[2] Since then, I have spent hours getting to know his music and listening to his songs, which are many and varied. I'm now also a signed-up member of the Red Hand Files, Cave's website in which he responds, with intense honesty, to questions sent to him by members of the public. Cave offers a mesmerising exploration of questions relating to faith, art, music, freedom, grief, loss and almost any other subject you can think of, drawing candidly on his own life, work and ethic. *Faith, Hope and Carnage* has received many plaudits, all of which are warranted.

I'm a little envious of Cave's capacity to articulate his feelings and express the deepest, most profound experiences of what it is to be human, through both his music and his writings, which are awe-inspiring, utterly beautiful and captivating. He is not what most people would call a conventional Christian, but there is no doubt that he is a person of deep faith, as well as deep doubt, who doesn't shy away from the difficult questions but finds transformation through the darkest, most painful times. Nick Cave would definitely be among the three people I would have at that imaginary meal we sometimes discuss with friends, where you can invite anyone you want, dead or alive.

It's difficult for me to pick out one song, as many entrance and absorb me. It is certainly true that some are easier to listen to than others; some require knowing more about what lies behind them, what inspired their writing and what the lyrics are conveying. For anyone who doesn't know Cave's music, 'Into My Arms' and the entire album it is from, *The Boatman's Call*, is probably a good place to start.[3] He wrote the track while he was in rehab and recollects:

They let you go to church on Sundays if you wanted to. I was actually walking back from church through the fields, and the tune came into my head, and when I got back to the facility I sat down at the cranky old piano and wrote the melody and the chords, then went up to the dormitory, sat on my bed and wrote the lyrics.[4]

'Into My Arms' is essentially a simple love ballad, full of pathos. It is sad and hopeful at the same time. It leans into the love and grace of Christ and it plays with the possibility that angels might still be real.

For reflection

1 Have you ever encountered an angel or had a mystical experience of any kind? If so, is it possible to describe what happened?
2 'God's glory, God's greatness and splendour, is simply and truly this: *God's love*.' Did this strike you in a fresh way? Do you agree?
3 Who might you draw alongside as a loving presence this week?

5

Fear and hope

It was the first Sunday after the new rector's installation at a friend's central London church, and the congregation was waiting rather nervously to discover what kind of priest they'd acquired. She began her sermon by asking, 'What are you most afraid of?' and my friend told me there was an almost audible sigh of relief. They'd got a pastor. They'd got somebody who understood.

Allowing ourselves to feel fearful

Fear can be paralysing. Yet it's a subject well worth grappling with, and in this chapter I'd like us to explore how acknowledging our fear – not denying or running away from it – can prove to be profoundly life-giving. Allowing ourselves to feel fearful, anxious and doubtful may be exactly what we need in order to begin to understand and experience the fruits of hope more fully.

Let's turn for a moment to someone who gets as close to the heart of what hope is as anyone I've come across: the playwright, poet and former political dissident Václav Havel. After the fall of the Iron Curtain, which led to the end of the Cold War and the dissolution of the Soviet Union, Havel became the first president of the newly formed Czech Republic in 1993. He spoke and wrote a great deal about hope, describing the connection between lacking and having hope like this: 'perhaps hopelessness is the very soil that nourishes human hope'.[1]

Fear and hope run like a thread throughout the entire Bible, across the full range of literary genres, including history, stories and parables, poetry and prophecies. Indeed, fear and hope are ever-present themes during the events of Advent and Christmas. 'Do not be afraid' is the opening rejoinder of the angels that appear respectively to Zechariah, Mary, Joseph and the shepherds. These are words of reassurance that take seriously the existence of fear. They offer comfort in the moment, not only acknowledging the alarm evoked by standing in the presence of an unknown heavenly being, but having deeper resonance too. 'Do not be troubled by the memory of past events,' they seem to say, 'nor about what the future may bring.'

I don't think we are expected to be fearless; we are, however, invited to resist the worst of what fear can do to us by holding on to hope. Yet it's difficult to define hope accurately or to talk about it in precise terms, because more than anything hope is *felt* and *experienced*. Václav Havel again:

> Hope is definitely not the same thing as optimism. It is not the conviction that something will turn out well, but the certainty that something makes sense, regardless of how it turns out … Hope, in this deep and powerful sense, is not the same as joy that things are going well, or willingness to invest in enterprises that are obviously headed for early success, but, rather,

an ability to work for something because it is good, not just because it stands a chance to succeed.[2]

For Havel, hope is 'a state of mind', 'a dimension of the soul' and 'an orientation of the spirit'.[3] We might say that hope is one of the melodies we most need to be attuned to.

Cultivating hope

Hope is certainly something that must be cultivated. In 1 Corinthians 13:13, Paul writes, 'Meanwhile these three remain: faith, hope, and love' (GNT). These are the Christian virtues we must practise in order to live well, and hope is, perhaps, the most neglected of the three. We instinctively seem to understand that love and faith are sometimes an act of will – we cannot love only when the mood takes us, and we strive to stay strong in faith even when tested. The same persistent determination is required of hope too, though we may not always recognise this.

I often think back to the conversations I had a few years ago with two priests who had been on a working trip to Northern Ireland. They had met with people from both sides of the Republican and Unionist divide, and both expressed to me (separately) how they had come away with a real lack of hope for the future of the province (this was well after the Good Friday Agreement of 1998). Yet neither said anything to suggest they struggled to love the people who held such extreme views, or how it had shaken their faith to see such deep animosity between Christians. I doubt these sentiments would have occurred to them. But they all too easily expressed their lack of hope. The truth is that if it is to make a difference, if it is to impact our lives and shape who we are, we must nurture hopefulness every day, just as we must nurture love and faith. Our hope may seem very small and dangerously fragile at times, but if tended carefully it can grow, just like the mustard seed in Jesus' parable. And gradually we might find that hope is capable of transforming pain and holding fear at bay.

Interrupt anxiety with gratitude

Perhaps it might be helpful here to mention another virtue: thankfulness. It's a long time since I came across the phrase 'interrupt anxiety with gratitude', and I have no recollection of where or when it was. But it made an enormous impact on me, and though I'm not always good at putting this excellent advice into practice, I frequently try to remind myself of it. And it does make a difference. Many of the things we feel anxious about are things we cannot actually control; no amount of fretful worrying will make them go away. So when I wake in the morning with a feeling of panic in the pit of my stomach, or when anxiety is eating away at me and I feel overcome with fear of what may or may not happen in the future, I intentionally try to detach a little and bring to mind one or two things that I'm grateful for. It's not that the fears magically disappear, but being reminded of the blessings in my life helps me gain a sense of perspective.

Sometimes we need to search actively for signs of hope; to lift our eyes, observe and notice. The prophet Ezekiel was part of the first generation of exiles in Babylon, around 600 years before the birth of Jesus. As someone who has lived in exile for most of my life, I feel an affinity with him, and I often look to Ezekiel for inspiration and insight. In his twenty-five years of exile, he had stared desolation in the face and experienced every kind of loss. Yet as he contemplates his fate and the fate of Israel, we don't find him giving in to self-pity and despondency. Rather, because he is practised in the art of hope, he notices something that would be so easy to miss: a trickle of water flowing out from below the temple. As he follows it, he sees how this insignificant trickle gradually grows to become a small stream and then a deep river. And his hope-filled eyes notice that where this river flows everything lives (Ezekiel 47).

Like Ezekiel we are called to be people of hope, to be those who spot the signs of God's presence in our world, our communities, our churches and our relationships. And having noticed, we are then to cherish and grow this hope, foster and practise it, even against the odds.

Confronting our fears

However, if hope is not to be some hollow fancy, first we must articulate our fears and look them in the eye. This is demanding work, and it may feel difficult to know where to begin. Perhaps we might start by writing down the anxieties that seem to cast a shadow over our day-to-day life. Maybe mixed in with those there is loss – something that once was but is no more – and we need to grieve.

There is good biblical precedence for this kind of process. The Lamentations of Jeremiah, the story of Job, and many of the psalms, to name a few, give voice, communally and individually, to pain, frustration and anxiety. When we cannot find our own words, they help us to lament, to vent and express our fear and hurt and anger. We can rest assured that God, who is bigger than all we can ever imagine, will be neither damaged nor offended by our lamenting. Rather, just like a mother holds and comforts a distraught child, so God holds and comforts us.

And in that comforting, it may be that we find ourselves challenged to become agents of transformation; to choose, notwithstanding our fear, to harness hope and use it for good. Although, as I've mentioned, there are matters we have no control over, there are other things we can work to change, whether within ourselves, like our attitudes and behaviours, or in the world around us. Protesting against injustices, small and large, takes courage, but as Nelson Mandela reputedly remarked, courage is not the absence of fear but the triumph over it.

This too is a seasonal theme, and I'd like to expand on it a little.

Christmas Tree festivals

I'm not sure if it's my imagination, but Christmas Tree festivals seem to be more popular than ever. You know the kind of thing – churches inviting individuals and groups from across their community to decorate and display a Christmas tree, providing an opportunity to bring people together, raise money for charity and celebrate Christmas, as well as the talents of those who participate.

In my mind, creating a dazzling display used to be what people aimed for. But these days it's touching to see how much creativity is being invested, with trees often saying something profound about those who have produced them. They can be a form of self-expression or a statement about priorities, whether of an individual or a group, or even a call to action. I've seen trees dressed with cut-out shapes traced around the hands of school children; knitted angels made by the Mothers' Union; buttons, bows and patchwork squares expertly fashioned by a local haberdashery shop; poppies contributed by the British Legion, and much more. Recently, I've been struck by the imaginative way participants have managed to stop us in our tracks. One tree I saw was festooned with plastic bottles and cans in a cry of protest against the waste that is destroying our planet; another, brought by the local Food Bank, was made entirely from cans of baked beans. 'We don't need any more baked beans!' the display seemed to be screaming, in a protest against the injustices of poverty that also issued a challenge: 'Don't just root around the back of your cupboards and bring us whatever comes to hand – please be a little more generous and thoughtful.'

Rebellion against the ways of the world

This led me to thinking about Advent and Christmas as a time for courageous protest – a strange idea at first, perhaps, but maybe something worth exploring. For is there not a protest of sorts at the heart of the Christmas story? We see God breaking into human history in a demonstration of gentle rebellion against the ways of the world. While the world tears itself apart in violence and hatred, God asserts his love for creation by becoming incarnate. While the world seeks the ways of wealth and influence, God is born in a humble stable, upholding the way of vulnerability and weakness. While kings and governors seek to rule with power, God follows the path of service and self-giving.

I love the lights and tinsel, the nativity plays and the gifts under the tree as much as the next person – truly I do. These are good things for us to enjoy. But let us never forget that the real story of Christmas is about a divine protest that also issues a challenge, asking how we too will participate and join the demonstration. Advent and Christmas urge us to consider what needs to change and what it is that prevents us from playing our part and joining the dance of rebellion against the status quo in favour of a transformed and better future.

So I invite you now to take a moment to consider what action you might take this season (and as I speak to you, dear reader, I speak of course to myself too). I'm not suggesting you try to impact the whole world – only the small part you inhabit. Perhaps as you do your Christmas shopping you could stop for a few minutes to talk to a homeless person and offer a hot drink or words of friendship. Or consider publicly standing up for a colleague or neighbour you think is being treated unfairly. Or take the time to sit and have a proper conversation with that annoying relative on Christmas Day. Or make a stand and gently refuse to play the part your family always expects of you, but which diminishes who you really are. Or write to your MP about issues that matter to you. Or, if you have a public platform of any kind, use it well and speak moderately and gently for justice, kindness and integrity, letting your actions be in accord with your words. It's with small incremental changes like these, through which we confront our fears and challenge our instinct for self-preservation, that glimpses of God's promise for a better future are drawn into the present moment.

May we hear the whisper of the angels this Christmas, and listen to their wisdom, put our fears aside and join the protest!

Philip Stopford: 'Do Not Be Afraid'

The unaccompanied choral piece 'Do Not Be Afraid' by the British composer Philip Stopford is based on words from Isaiah 43:1–4:

Do not fear, for I have redeemed you;
I have called you by name, you are mine.
When you pass through the waters, I will be with you;

> and through the rivers, they shall not overwhelm
> you;
> when you walk through fire you shall not be burned,
> and the flame shall not consume you.
> For I am the LORD your God,
> … you are precious in my sight,
> and honoured, and I love you.

The anthem was commissioned for the baptism of Andrew and Kathryn Radley's baby daughter in 2010 and was first performed at St Peter and St Paul's Church, Uplyme. It was written for mixed choir, with soprano solo, and like much of Stopford's music it is melodic and memorable, comprising rich and sometimes unexpected textures. The gentle but persistent repetition of the phrase 'do not fear' has a calming effect, while the harmonies express something of the underlying tensions and uncertainties that lurk despite the reassuring words. There is a magical moment about three minutes into the piece when the music suddenly opens up with a surge of hopefulness, and the treble solo, near the end, soars above the choir to reiterate the central message and carry us to another realm.

For reflection

1 What are you most afraid of? If this seems too scary to articulate, is there someone you might turn to for help?
2 How might you nurture hopefulness every day?

('Interrupt anxiety with gratitude' is encouragingly
practical.)

3 '... the real story of Christmas is about a divine protest
that also issues a challenge, asking how we too will
participate and join the demonstration.' What might
you do this Advent to help bring in the kingdom of
God?

6

Reconciliation

In Chapter 4, I reflected a little on the signs that the angels pointed to when they appeared to the shepherds on the hillside. They sang of God's glory and love and of 'good news that will cause great joy for all the people'. Notably, the angels also sang of peace: 'Glory to God in the highest heaven, and on earth peace among those whom he favours' (Luke 2:14). Indeed, the whole of the Gospel of Luke is framed by this proclamation of peace. It is here as Jesus' birth is announced, and again in the final days of his life as the crowds greet him on his entry into Jerusalem, crying out, 'Blessed is the king who comes in the name of the Lord! Peace in heaven and glory in the highest heaven!' (Luke 19:38). The angels' voices at his birth merge with those of the throng before his impending death to proclaim one extraordinary song: this is the King, the King who brings peace.

Longing for peace

And yet this peace is so often missing from the world presented to us daily in the news. As I write, there is little sign of the conflicts in Ukraine and Israel/Palestine abating. Demonstrations continue to erupt from time to time in cities across Iran, stories keep emerging about the appalling treatment of women in Afghanistan, thousands are dying in South Sudan and, in Britain, we are still reeling from the riots that followed the murder of innocent children in Southport in the summer of 2024. And if, occasionally, these atrocities take a back seat, there are likely to be others filling our screens.

I often find my thoughts turning to the angels singing of peace over Bethlehem. If you visit that holy place today, you will likely see shepherds and babies; you will probably also see a wise person or two. But where, I wonder, is the heavenly host? We so badly need to hear the angels' song.

Of course, peace is not just the absence of war. Admittedly, if you look for dictionary definitions you will find explanations like 'freedom from disturbance', 'tranquillity', 'a state or period in which there is no war or war has ended'. Yet those don't quite capture the whole meaning. When Middle Easterners greet one another with *Shalom* or *Salaam*, they are saying so much more. In its fullest sense, peace expresses something about healthy and enduring relationships, of living harmoniously with one another and the whole of creation, in mutuality, warmth and integration; it speaks of inner serenity and stillness. This kind of peace is not so much about removing difficulties or challenges, but about how these are navigated, with gentleness, calmness and hope, regardless of what is going on around us. True peace, then, is about *reconciliation* – the restoring to wholeness of that which is harmed, damaged or broken. True peace involves being reconciled to ourselves, to one another, to creation and to God.

Israel and Palestine

In the world as it presently is, reconciliation is arguably what individuals and communities need more than anything else. It is so frustratingly obvious and yet so very hard to achieve. On a couple of recent trips to Israel and Palestine, the full force of this hit home as I came to understand a little more about the complex history of that place and its people. I had previously visited the region several times, but not for many years. This time I was there on two occasions not long after the Hamas attack of 7 October 2023, in which several hundred Israelis were brutally massacred and many were taken hostage. Subsequently, Israel responded with its own violent and ruthless attack on Gaza. Reports to date suggest that since the war began, over 50,000 civilians have been killed, nearly two million have been displaced and much of the region's farmland and infrastructure has been destroyed. These statistics are staggering and it's hard to imagine that behind them lie countless individual stories, lives devastated, hopes and dreams shattered, and with ripple effects going far and wide, impacting many more and threatening peace in the wider Middle East.

The purpose of both my brief trips was to show support for, and solidarity with, the Anglican Diocese in Jerusalem and also to listen and learn; to try to understand a little more about the situation from the perspective of those who live there. They were intense experiences, during which I met with a wide range of individuals, ordinary civilians and those representing different groups and projects.

Among them were people from several NGOs, Palestinian Christians in the West Bank, and representatives from Rabbis for Human Rights. I received warm hospitality as I listened and listened, hearing many heart-breaking stories that moved me to tears.

A sense of helplessness

The courage and commitment I witnessed was inspiring, yet I came away with a sense of my own utter helplessness, feeling I had nothing worthwhile to offer in the face of unutterable pain. Nonetheless, I resolved to speak out a little more for peace with justice – for reconciliation. The problems in this region that is so central to the stories of Advent and Christmas are intractable. They involve deep and historic sensitivities that leave many of us fearful of saying the wrong thing. But as Christians, surely it is right that we speak out against injustice wherever we see it? The Hamas attack was shocking and despicable and should be condemned, and so too has been the extent of the Israeli offensive in Gaza where ordinary people in their thousands are suffering untold misery, and where the international community is largely turning a blind eye and continuing to provide arms to Israel.

Much of this I think I already knew before my trip, but I absorbed it with a new force through being present, meeting with people and hearing their personal stories. Of all the things that struck me, however, the most significant was undoubtedly the lack of any real and meaningful connection between the opposing sides. Each listens to its own news channels; each is trapped in its own narrative, its own sense of identity, its own version of history and truth. I was reminded of parallel tracks, where never the twain shall meet.

Yet for there to be any chance of lasting peace and reconciliation, it will be necessary at some point for those on opposing sides – especially those in positions of power – to demonstrate a willingness to imagine life from the other's perspective.

There are, of course, good and brave people working for change in Israel and Palestine, striving to create opportunities for deeper understanding across the divides and pave the way for reconciliation. Among those I met from Rabbis for Human Rights was Rabbi Michael Murmur, his wife Sarah Bernstein from the Rossling Centre for Interreligious Education, and Salim Munayer, founder of Musalaha. The last is a Christian organisation that teaches reconciliation to mixed groups of Israelis and Palestinians through facilitated training sessions and an extensive six-step programme. The long-held and deeply ingrained perspectives and prejudices on each side make the work of Musalaha enormously challenging and many don't make it through the course, falling away when it becomes too hard to stay. The pull of our own stories and histories, our own vision of the world, is very powerful indeed. But Munayer's persistence is inspiring and clearly makes a difference, modelling an alternative way and holding out the possibility of hope for a better future. Listening to him, it was impossible not to hear the music emanating from the depths of his soul, singing of a deep and raw pain, longing for transformation.[1]

An interlude

Recently I attended a performance of Benjamin Britten's *War Requiem* at the Royal Albert Hall. This remarkable work was commissioned to mark the consecration of Coventry's new cathedral in May 1962 after the previous one had been destroyed in the Blitz. Britten intersperses the traditional Latin text of the Requiem Mass with nine of Wilfred Owen's war poems emanating from his experiences in the First World War. The music and words combine to ensure we do not forget the devastating losses of both world wars. This is how the programme notes describe its power: '[The work] resonates beyond its own time and place, spreading its compelling pacifist message in a world still riven by conflict … It has a simple and direct pacifist message, yet also embodies a complex act of commemoration. It is both a memorial and a warning.'[2]

The importance of creativity

Artists who challenge and inspire, bringing joy and helping us face pain, are not optional extras; they are essential for any civilised society to flourish. In July 2024, during the conflict in Gaza, letters from Palestinian children in the region were handed to 10 Downing Street by the international development charity Christian Aid, as part of a renewed appeal for an immediate ceasefire. I was very struck by one letter from Mais Abdel Hadi, President of the Palestinian Children's Council. Amid the utter devastation of everything that makes up normal life, as people were living in indescribable conditions and in constant fear for their lives, Hadi expressed a longing for the ordinary things that bring delight. This is what she wrote: 'Stop the death by starvation, the killing by denying medicine, and the destruction of health centres. Bring back life through songs, poems and music. We are children who hope for a dignified life and do not wish for anyone to suffer.'[3]

'Songs, poems and music' are the things that make for a healthy, peaceful and free society. It is no wonder that in despotic and dictatorial regimes they are among the first things to be denied or repressed, for artists can evoke fear in the hearts of the powerful.

A society without creativity is a pale shadow of how human beings should live.

Peace and reconciliation

As I said at the beginning of this chapter, the angels remind us that the baby soon to be born pleads with us to take seriously the message of peace and reconciliation. It must reverberate through all our relationships: with those who are like us and those who are different, those we agree with and those we disagree with, those we love and those we can't stand.

Lest we think these are nice but ineffective sentiments, let me spell out the challenge. Peace and goodwill – a willingness to reconcile those relationships that are broken – must permeate our Advent and Christmas whatever it looks like and whoever we are forced to share it with. It must soak into the time we spend with those relatives who are more welcome when they leave than when they arrive; it must infuse the family rift that has festered due to the unspoken apology or undeclared hurt.

Can we not hear the music of the soul gently beckoning us to put all bitterness aside and see the sign, vulnerable and laid for us in a manger?

I hear it said, in the Church especially, that truth is of greater importance than unity and that we should be more worried about siding with truth than promoting reconciliation. But can any of us really claim to possess the truth? Isn't the good news of the gospel a truth that cannot easily be contained or fully understood, because ultimately God's love and God's truth are beyond our comprehension? Perhaps it is better to think of ourselves as faithful seekers after truth, rather than those who fully possess it. Perhaps truth is not ours to own but ours continually to pursue. Further still, perhaps truth in its fullest sense is not about specific beliefs or doctrines at all, but about a way of living as described by the apostle Paul in Colossians 3 when he says, 'clothe yourselves with compassion, kindness, humility, meekness, patience' (v. 12). And, he goes on, 'teach and admonish one another in all wisdom' (v. 16). What would it be like in our communities if we admonished one another for not living and teaching *this* truth, this clothing of ourselves with compassion, kindness, humility and so on?

In the end, we cannot be reconciled to anyone else until first we are at peace with ourselves – with all that has shaped us and brought us to this place, knowing our shortcomings but aware too that these need no longer define us or our future. I must recognise my own capacity for wrongdoing and for causing hurt; my propensity for pride and envy, even violence – in thought and word, if not in deed. And as I recognise these things, I have to live with the contradiction of knowing too that I am loved beyond measure, forgiven and held by the one who is God-made-flesh, accepting that this is not about ignoring injustice or bad behaviour, but about understanding that Jesus' offer of peace breaks into the ordinariness of our lives and seeps into everything we do. It is about living lives that are orientated towards the way of reconciliation.

None of this is easy or without pain. Reconciliation might involve many years of struggle, of anger and frustration laid bare. In his book *The Language of Tears,* David Runcorn reminds us of the oft-misunderstood and undervalued place of tears in our lives.[4] Many, especially Western men, are strangers to their own tears. Most of us will be familiar with attempts to resist them and hold back the tide, embarrassed and apologetic for fear that people will think us weak. In truth, 'tears go with being a creature who wonders, who longs and who feels things'.[5] They are an intrinsic part of who we are. They have a language of their own, and in learning to understand this, we will come to know ourselves better. Our tears connect us with our deepest emotions and prayers, and can drive us to action. Paradoxically, they can help us see more clearly. Though our vision is temporarily obscured by them, the things that matter most come into sharper focus. Through our tears, we see the world's injustices and pain, but we also see its beauty and splendour, and these can open the way towards healing and reconciliation.

Beauty restored

My childhood home in Isfahan was the bishop's house, which belonged to the Diocese of Iran. I lived there from birth, and it was the place where my earliest memories were forged and where I felt safe and secure. In 1980, around the time my family and I were forced into exile, the house and many other properties and institutions belonging to the church were unlawfully confiscated by the authorities, along with everything inside them. For a long time, the home I loved sat vacant and unused, an empty shell of a building, and though there was much talk that it would be used to support the *mostazafan* – the poor and oppressed – nothing ever happened ...

Until a couple of years ago, when we received news that the property had been turned into a museum housing vestiges of Iran's past and present, and is now open to the public. It remains the case that our home was commandeered illegally and the injustice of that still stings; indeed, it is hard to reconcile. But there is some comfort in knowing that the building once more has a purpose, and its beauty has been restored. I have watched the brief promotional video and it takes me through the contours of the house, from one room to another.[6] Most are unrecognisable in their detail, but some are searingly familiar; the entrance to my father's study, for example, and the staircase where I would sit as a little girl, near the top, when I was meant to be in bed, listening to the sounds of hospitality downstairs. I hope and pray that the museum will bring joy to many.

David Runcorn, quoting Simon Parke, says:

> Resignation is the angry admission that I cannot get my own way; surrender is the peaceful acceptance that 'my own way' cannot be separated from the rest of reality. Resignation is the attitude of the ego, the separate self, thwarted by reality and resentfulness. Surrender lets go of such wilfulness, and the idea that the future must conform to my wishes.[7]

Recognising and appreciating the *beauty* of the museum that now occupies my former home has helped me move from a place of resignation to a place of surrender. And if beauty has helped me move from resignation to surrender, it has also paved the way for a deeper sense of reconciliation.

When I'm presiding at a service of Holy Communion, at the end of the Eucharistic Prayer I hold up the priest's wafer and break it, saying the words: 'We break this bread to share in the body of Christ ...' As I look out to the congregation through the space between the two halves of the wafer, and they look back at me, there is both beauty and brokenness, perhaps even beauty *in* brokenness. The wonder of the first is all the more pronounced where there is the second, and we experience this most profoundly when we share bread and wine, the body and blood of Christ, broken and shed for us, inviting us to surrender, gently beckoning us towards the place of reconciliation.

Sinead O'Connor: 'Take Me to Church'

'Take Me to Church' by Sinead O'Connor is the penultimate track on her 2014 album *I'm not Bossy, I'm the Boss*, and it was another of my choices for *Desert Island Discs*. There had to be something from the Irish singer! My husband is from Northern Ireland and a huge fan of hers. Over the years, he's given me a love for her music and, indeed, for many things Irish.

Sinead O'Connor was an immensely gifted and influential musician who died far too young, at the age of fifty-six, in 2023. Not only did she sing and write songs, O'Connor was also a political activist, especially vocal in her support of a united Ireland, and never shy of controversy. To many she seemed a tortured soul, unremitting and restless in her search for meaning, which led her to explore a wide range of mainstream and more unconventional religious traditions. Allyson McCabe's book, *Why Sinéad O'Connor Matters*, published since the singer's death, is a thoughtful study of a fascinating and provocative life.[8] O'Connor's songs are relentlessly real, gritty and honest – she had no time for sentimentality. She will undoubtedly leave her mark for a very long time to come, both on the music industry and on the many who loved and appreciated her work.

As well as being a great song, 'Take Me to Church' serves as a reminder that the Church, which should be a place of healing and reconciliation, has all too often been one of pain and hurt. That is certainly how Sinead O'Connor experienced it, and shamefully it is true for many others too. The work of reconciliation can often only begin when the powerful are honest, repentant and willing to change.

For reflection

1 When did you last feel prompted to consider a situation from someone else's perspective? (This may have happened in your head – they may not have been aware you were struggling at all.)

2 There are many ways to express creativity and help society flourish – for example, through music, writing, photography, craftwork, gardening. How do you express yours?

3 Can you think of a time in your life when 'beauty in brokenness' seemed particularly relevant and/or healing?

7

Silence and darkness

We come now to a theme perhaps more traditionally associated with Advent than some of the others we have explored: darkness. And I've chosen to couple it with its counterpart, silence. Darkness and silence point towards places we are often frightened to go to, experiences we would rather avoid, spaces from which we try to flee. But in this chapter, we will seek to grow in understanding by dwelling with darkness and leaning into silence. To enter darkness and silence fully, to experience what they have to offer, we must cultivate the capacity for patience, for living with uncertainty, confusion and pain; in short, if darkness and silence are to do their work, we must learn how to wait.

Admittedly, this will not be easy. Silence, darkness and waiting are not concepts readily embraced by contemporary Western culture: we are relentlessly surrounded by sound and assaulted by bright lights and, increasingly, what we need or want is often available at the touch of a button. Everything from books to takeaway meals, from toys to household goods, from medication to train tickets can now be ordered from the comfort of our living room, without any need for human interaction.

Finding meaning in the waiting

Moreover, smart phones and all manner of other electronic devices make it easy to distract ourselves from the more difficult aspects of daily living. We can, if we choose, avoid facing the darkness and silence of our sadnesses, losses, frailties and regrets – at least for a while. In the end, we will never escape. As many astute souls have learned before us, it's wiser to stop, dwell awhile and make friends with the darkness and silence. Hopefully, we will discover, little by little, that there is meaning in the waiting (to borrow R. S. Thomas's resonant phrase[1]). It is not a waste of time; it is not something simply to be tolerated until the next thing comes along to distract us. For in the darkness and silence and sometimes painful waiting, we are being shaped and formed; we are learning more about ourselves and about the God who loves us.

Theologians Silvianne and Barnabas Aspray write about this eloquently in one of my favourite online journals, *Seen & Unseen*, and they take it up a notch, moving beyond how we might deal with our problems and emotions, to the need to discover our sense of place and rootedness in the universe. Modern life, say the Asprays, distracts us from asking and pondering the big questions of life, the very questions we should be attending to: 'We are wealthy, comfortable, bombarded with entertainment, and often very busy with careers and children as well. All these things help us to repress the deeper questions about the origin and purpose of our existence.' The Asprays refer to the 'narcotic of everyday life' – the ways in which daily existence and society act as a drug to cloud our vision, confuse our thinking and prevent us from honestly facing up to the things that matter most.[2]

Being too distracted to make time for deep contemplation means that we are (often unthinkingly) making decisions, both small and large, based on values that reveal what we regard as important. We do not pause amid the hubbub, breathe deeply and ponder: what actually are the values on which I want to build my life?

Journeying towards the truth

While I believe that faith can put us on the right track, I don't think that Christianity provides a set of neat and easy answers to the challenges we face, and the Bible isn't a moral code book, offering solutions to all our ethical dilemmas (handy though that might be). Rather, we are invited to step into the story of salvation and, as part of the Christian community, to journey towards the truth. This will involve ceasing our activity and busyness, and entering the darkness and the silence that constantly draw our attention back to the things that may not be easy or comfortable, but matter most profoundly. It involves listening to the music of the soul.

How do we listen well? By this stage in the book you may well feel you've heard quite a lot about this. But bear with me. The fact is that though listening is such an important part of life and our relationships, we don't tend to give it much thought. On the whole, most of us are better at talking than listening. We want our point of view to be heard, and even when we're attending to others, we're often focusing more on what we might say next. Psychologists refer to different levels or degrees of listening. If you do a Google search, there are, according to different people, anywhere between four and seven, but in each case the principle is that to *truly* listen – deeply and attentively – you have to be empathetic; you must have the ability to put yourself into the shoes of the other, to see the world from their perspective; to be non-judgemental. Listening in such a way is a skill that can be learned and developed.

Our tendency towards self-obsession (for that's what it really comes down to) is reflected in our relationship with God as well. We can be quite good at talking *to* God, bringing our requests and praying for people. But the idea of making time simply to listen to God is something else entirely. Crucially, to do it well we have to be patient; we have to practise and put in place spiritual disciplines that may require many years to hone.

However, before we go further, perhaps it's fair to ask why we might want to listen to God. Why might it be important? Well, we've already touched on the search for meaning and connection. But alongside that, surely as Christians and people of faith we are always seeking the will of God in our lives and in the world; we want to align ourselves with God's mission and be those who contribute to the building of God's kingdom.

Unlike the listening that takes place within our human relationships, the normal rules don't apply when listening to God. Except in rare instances experienced by a small number of people, most of us don't hear the voice of God literally, so the use of language is somewhat redundant. Fortunately, the *desire* to listen, the act of *intentionally giving time*, the commitment to *bringing ourselves* to the place of listening again and again, even though we are often distracted and seem to be failing – these are sufficient for God, who is ever present and longs for us to draw near.

Hearing God's voice

There is, of course, no single (non-literal) way of hearing God's voice. We are offered myriad opportunities – through communing with nature, engaging with the insights of others and reading Scripture, to name but three. These all require a willingness to have our assumptions challenged, a readiness to embrace the unexpected and surprising. In faith, it seems to me, we are often searching for clarity and simplicity, but we cannot find it without first engaging with the mysterious and the complex. Oliver Wendell Holmes, the nineteenth-century physician, poet and polymath, and man of many quotes, is reputed to have said: 'For the simplicity on this side of complexity, I wouldn't give you a fig. But for the simplicity on the other side of complexity, for that I would give you anything I have.'

However, willing though we may be to try to move through complexity towards the simplicity of hearing God's voice, it's not easy. We might miss the divine utterance amid the many distractions, the din of noises within and without. Remember Elijah, in 1 Kings 19: he strained to hear God's voice on Mount Horeb, in the storm, the earthquake and the fire, before eventually discerning it as a quiet whisper. Only after the turmoil did God speak to Elijah and make clear the way ahead. Simplicity emerged out of much complexity, and it came amid 'a sound of sheer silence' (v. 12).

This story offers reassurance that there is a place in the life of faith for cultivating our capacity for silence before God. The discipline of regularly coming with no agenda other than to listen, usually referred to as contemplative prayer, has become increasingly important in my own faith journey. You'd think it would be straightforward: desist from activity, be still and give God a chance to speak into your heart and mind. Yet it turns out to be incredibly hard. Let me reveal what tends to happen during my daily routine.

The challenges of silence

First, I take myself somewhere quiet and try to clear my mind by setting aside my priorities and concerns and deliberately stepping into the silence. Quickly there are interruptions – and I don't mean from the world around me. Rather, it is always my ego that accompanies the thoughts that pour into the silence – what *I* might do or say or think, as I play over scenarios and conversations in my mind. As well as trying to sidestep my ego, I also try to stop telling God stuff. (There's a time and place for that in intercessory prayer, when we bring the needs of the world and the people we care about and lay before God our innermost hopes and desires.)

I'm told that Archbishop Rowan Williams was once asked, during an interview, about his spiritual disciplines.

He told the reporter that he prayed for an hour every morning, which prompted the reporter to ask, 'And what do you say to God?'

'Very little,' said Williams. 'I listen for around fifty-five minutes and then spend five minutes telling God about those things that are on my heart.'

I'm not sure how accurate this story is, but it contains much wisdom and sounds like the kind of thing Archbishop Rowan might well have said.

If at this point you feel like despairing, let me also share this comforting story told of Thomas Keating, one of the great modern proponents and practitioners of contemplative prayer. Keating was sought out by many who came to him for spiritual direction. On a particular occasion, one of his mentees complained bitterly that he simply couldn't do this contemplative prayer stuff and that every time he tried, a hundred thoughts would intervene. Keating saw it differently. 'How wonderful,' he said. 'A hundred opportunities to draw your attention back towards God.' These are words to hearten anyone who wishes to explore the silence of God but feels frustrated by their own shortcomings.

As for the question of what we're listening for when we come to God in silence, I'm not sure that the answer has anything much to do with specific responses to questions or concerns we may have, because that, again, would relate to our own preoccupations. The silence is more about wasting time with God as we might with a friend or loved one. It's about developing and strengthening a relationship, putting in place habits that will sustain us through the storms of life.

Crucially for me, contemplative prayer has been about surrendering my worries and anxieties, acknowledging my lack of control and trusting that God will guide me one step at a time. I am learning that I don't need to know the results of all my efforts, or all the answers as to how things are going to turn out. I don't need to spend unnecessary time worrying about matters beyond my power. Rather, I take responsibility where I can and beyond that seek the unfolding of God's will, asking for wisdom, courage and compassion enough for today. In short, this daily discipline of bringing myself before God for as little as fifteen minutes or so is about learning the art of surrender. And I feel that I have changed, over time. Not that I've become a better person or that I never worry (though I wish both of these were true). Rather, I am able to tilt my life a little more towards God, to know my place and my size in the scheme of things, and on the whole this has been liberating.

Over a hundred years ago, in a passage that seems uncannily contemporary, the mystic Evelyn Underhill expressed things like this:

If we are to find and feel the Eternal, we must give time and place to it in our lives – a desperate modern need in too many busy, hurried lives. Such recollection – a gathering up of our interior forces and retreat of consciousness to its 'ground' – is the preparation of all great endeavour. It's more productive of strength to spend that odd ten minutes in the morning in feeling and finding the Eternal, than in flicking through the newspaper. This will send us off to the day's work properly orientated, gathered together, recollected and really endowed with new power of dealing with each circumstance.[3]

The power of darkness

Having addressed the value of silence, let us turn our attention towards darkness and ask if that too might be worth exploring.

A couple of years ago I visited Sweden for a few days in early December, where in common with other Scandinavian countries Advent is a big deal. The days are short and the evenings long, and the Swedes seem to embrace the night. Rather than trying to overpower it with bright and gaudy illuminations, they welcome the darkness and lace it gently with soft candlelight. This may make for pretty sights and romantic settings, yet it somehow also has the effect of enhancing the power of darkness, reminding us of the theological reality that the darkness has a beauty and purpose of its own.

I'd like to explore this further by speaking of one of the most memorable books I've read in recent years, *Learning to Walk in the Dark* by the American priest and theologian Barbara Brown Taylor,[4] a prolific and bestselling author with a gift for uncovering profound truths amid the ordinariness of life. This volume had an especially significant impact on me, perhaps because I read it during lockdown, when the world was going through its own particular kind of Covid pandemic darkness. Brown Taylor challenged me to rethink and reframe the idea of darkness and its relationship with the light (I will say more on this in the following chapter). She reminds us that when God created the heavens and the earth, darkness was not eradicated. It stayed, in the form of night and in contrast to the day. If God thought darkness was worth keeping, then surely it can't be all bad, can it? She reminds us that good things happen under the cover of darkness: babies grow in the womb and we get the sleep we need to stay mentally and physically well, for example. If it wasn't for the darkness, we would never be able to see the beauty of the stars; and the resurrection took place in the darkness of a tomb. Before Christ broke out into the light, whatever happened to turn death into life took place in the dark.

One particularly memorable illustration is the story Brown Taylor tells of an occasion when she went caving with a friend to experience the quality of darkness you only get in chambers made of rock. As they travelled deeper and deeper into the heart of the cave with nothing more than a watery torchlight to guide their footsteps, they sometimes had to feel their way, edging along the side, stumbling as they went – a dangerous activity and not one for the faint-hearted. Before returning to the world outside, Brown Taylor broke off the edge of a glistening piece of rock that had caught her eye, taking it as a memento of her day. Back in the sunlight she was disappointed to see that what she had thought was a gem was, in fact, just an ordinary bit of stone – nothing special and no longer sparkling. It was the power of darkness, with just the tiniest help from a passing torch, that had made it sparkle like a precious jewel; its beauty was lost in the broad light of day.

I have shared this story many times at the licensing of new clergy in their parishes. I remind them (and in the process myself) that we should, of course, all continue to shine our own particular God-given light, but in doing so we mustn't forget the darkness. For all of us will at some point encounter darkness and are likely to be alongside others in the darknesses they carry. We cannot, and indeed should not, always try to cast the kind of light that seeks to shatter the darkness and evade the pain. Instead, if we have the courage and tenacity to walk patiently through the darkness, with enough light cast by tender acts of kindness, then mysteriously we may just uncover fresh insights and discover the meaning of love in new and deeper ways.

Contemplating death

Our natural fear of silence and darkness, and our instinct to try to avoid them, might partly arise from their association with death and what lies beyond it – whether we happen to think of this as a vast nothingness, or the place we expect to encounter the judgement of God. It may seem a little tenuous, but consider this for a moment: every time we switch off the lights and lay down in our beds to sleep, we are embarking on an ending of sorts. We enter the silence and the darkness of the night, dying to that which has been and not knowing what tomorrow will bring. We are alone with our thoughts and our longings; fears loom large as our innermost selves are laid bare before God, who alone knows the truth of our lives.

In the normal course of events, the instinct to cling to life is powerful and strong, even if we're not exactly fearful of death. I've already mentioned my mother's final days. She was a woman of deep and profound faith who had lived a generous and gentle, even saintly, life. And yet the task of letting go in order to be embraced by the silence of death and the 'dazzling darkness' of God, which Henry Vaughan invites us to contemplate in his poem 'The Night', was not straightforward. As she became weaker and weaker, she clung on with a tenacity that was both astonishing and characteristic.

I have often reflected on this and wonder if what most of us desire, when we think about death, is a good ending at the culmination of a long life, preferably painless, with loved ones nearby, a clear conscience, and hope for what is to follow beyond. Not everyone is granted such an ending, and many suffer grievously. This reality is part of the cruelty of the world that is so difficult to comprehend.

Dvořák: Cello concerto in B minor, Op. 104

Antonin Dvořák wrote his concerto for cello and orchestra in B minor in 1894. I have always loved this piece – it arguably unlocked the way for many of the wonderful cello concertos that would follow. For me, this piece includes one of the greatest endings of all in the canon of classical music. Throughout the concerto, Dvořák used the full range of the cello, exposing its soul in a way that had not previously been done. In the process, he composed a work of genius that captures every human emotion, combining power with passion, melancholy with exquisite joy.

The third and final movement was a tribute to his sister-in-law, who was seriously ill and died shortly before the piece was first performed. After the richness and contrasts that make up the finale, the concerto draws to a close with a slow and wistful passage, fading like a breath, before the orchestra unexpectedly regains its full voice, carrying us swiftly and dramatically towards the triumphant conclusion.[5]

For reflection

1 How good are you at waiting? Are there particular circumstances in which it seems easier or harder to hold on patiently for things to unfold?
2 When or where do you feel closest to God?
3 Can you think of a time when darkness of a physical, mental or spiritual kind revealed unexpected insights?

8

Light and space

In the chapel at Bishopscourt, the home of the Bishop of Chelmsford and where I currently live, there is a triptych of three small windows. The middle one, in brightly coloured stained glass, captures – through its curved contours and abstract patterns, shapes and symbols – elements of diocesan life. There are also allusions to Scripture, the Holy Trinity, the tree of life and the kingdom of God.[1] Etched on the two outer windows are words from the prologue to John's Gospel: *The light shines in the darkness, and the darkness has not overcome it.*

As we begin this chapter, I would like to reflect further on the interplay between light and darkness that we touched on briefly in the last chapter.

The co-existence of light and darkness

Let's start with the simple understanding that light and darkness are not mutually exclusive. As I mentioned in my introduction, it's tempting to get caught up in the binary way society looks at the world these days, but the truth is that light and darkness always co-exist, in an uneasy but necessary tension. Their interplay provides fertile soil for creativity, and if we are willing to embrace the patterns they create in our lives, we're likely to discover a lot more about what it means to be fully human.

Just think about how musicians and artists of every description work not only with colour and texture to produce contrasting images and sounds, but frequently play with light and shade too. A painter may use light, for example, to prompt us to focus on a particular detail of their composition; or in the way the light contrasts strikingly with darker elements, drawing attention to how the two interact and together generate something new. Similarly, musicians employ major and minor keys, high and low registers, harmonic dissonance and consonance to create dark and light. And when music, as an art form, is experienced in real time, the composer's gift is given life by the performer, who adds their own particular interpretation while beckoning listeners to discover the meaning of the piece for themselves.

So, for light to have space to shine, literally or metaphorically, it needs its counterpart. After all, without the darkness of the night, we would never experience the glory of the breaking dawn. From a slightly different perspective on this theme of light and dark, the twentieth-century Austrian conductor Herbert von Karajan is reputed to have remarked that greatness in anything must be preceded by suffering. Indeed, I have often heard it said of talented young musicians that, having mastered their technique, the only thing left to improve their playing is to experience the pain of a broken heart. Life is bittersweet; light and dark are closely bound in an often perplexing and enigmatic dance. Elsewhere, I have written about paradise gardens and how they are often situated in desert plains.[2] Their beauty comes partly from the contrast with the arid landscape around them.

Connecting in messiness

Let's turn again at this point to Mary who, as life-giver and bearer of God's Son, understood how pain and sorrow are inextricably bound together with the raptures of motherhood. In Luke 2, when Jesus is presented in the temple, the scene is one of 'unbounded joy'[3] as Simeon cradles the child in his arms and presents him to the Lord. But there is also a foreshadowing of the darkness to come, as Simeon addresses Mary directly and tells her of the sword that will pierce her soul. This is a darkness that must be passed through if the true light of the world is to shine; there is no bypassing the agony of crucifixion before resurrection life bursts forth. Looking at Mary reminds us too that the people who are dearest to us, who bring light into our lives, can also be the cause of our deepest anguish. The pain of loss, of broken relationships, betrayals, unfulfilled dreams, is all the more acute when we have experienced the joy and tenderness of love. The reverse is also true. When we are in the depths of despair, feeling enveloped by darkness and sorrow, the shafts of light that break through can feel all the more precious and wonderful. It is on these contradictions that our lives are built. Yet there is comfort in realising that it is often in the messiness that we find meaning and make the deepest connections with others whose lives are complex and messy too.

As Christians, we are called to be the light of Christ – both when that's easy and when it's hard. We are called, also, to *notice* the light and draw attention to it when it shines in unexpected and forgotten places. The birth of baby Jesus points each year, lest we should forget, to the hope of new beginnings and to the fulfilment of all our longings – to the time when every tear will be wiped from our eyes and the whole of creation will be reconciled to God. This joyful truth is music for the soul at the deepest level.

An expansive view of art

In thinking about light and how we encounter it in life, I find myself drawn to the idea of space, which is why, for this final chapter, I have linked two concepts that seem to belong with each other. Recently, I listened to an episode of *The Rest Is Politics (Leading)*, with the celebrated artist and sculptor Antony Gormley.[4] I was fascinated by the way he talked about the 'awareness of space' having been crucial to his development as an artist. 'I think of my work as being about space, not being about objects,' he said, 'and I'm interested in how you activate space.' Gormley seems less concerned about producing specific pieces of art than with the idea of animating spaces – creating 'a field effect' into which viewers are invited to participate and become part of the picture.

This wonderfully expansive view of art – as a bridge between people, crossing boundaries of gender, race, class and so on – perhaps has something to teach us about faith as well. So often we are tempted to define the truths of faith according to our own understanding or priorities. Different traditions cast their own particular light, producing specific versions of Christianity which, for those on the inside, become familiar and safe. Yet there is a constant danger that instead of inviting others into the space to animate it with their different experiences and perspectives, we are tempted to build walls to protect our truths, to contain them and keep them uncontaminated. In the process, we may seek to define and limit God by the narrowness of our own vision. In reality, God is beyond all our definitions and God's love will never be confined by our understanding.

'The poem became flesh ...'

Perhaps one of the reasons I'm drawn to the idea of spaciousness in faith is that, although I'm not a poet, I've long preferred to engage with faith more as if it were poetry than prose. So, you will not be surprised at my delight when I came across an article by Belle Tindall called 'The poem became flesh and dwelt among us'.[5] This has shaped my reflections further and I've drawn on Tindall's thoughts in this section.

Good poetry offers deep insights that are often illusive and difficult to capture precisely. It provides precious moments of clarity, in which everything seems to make perfect sense. At the same time, poetry has a tendency to dodge and disobey hard definitions. It plays back to us echoes of our soul music and connects us to the mysteries that provide meaning and purpose. Poetry makes profound sense of us, even if the truth it tries to convey cannot be wholly proven or pinned down or contained; it resonates in a way that is often hard to explain.

All these things may be said of Christian faith as well. Faith is expansive and hard to define. It helps make sense of our lives, takes us beyond the obvious, allows us to plummet the depths, to explore layers of meaning about ourselves and the universe. It propels us into the realm of mystery and invites us to open ourselves up to divine revelation. It provides space for exploration and encounter, room to ask questions, to draw closer, to catch glimpses of eternity, to inch towards knowing and understanding better the greatest poem of all, which is Jesus Christ. The Word became flesh and dwelt among us, John tells us, but Tindall takes this a step further and suggests that the Poem became flesh and is living among us.

Human beings have an innate capacity for poetry, and also an innate capacity for faith and for Jesus Christ. None of us has all the answers, but we are called gently and deliberately to make room for others who may be searching for answers too. How might we do this well, not just as individuals but as the Church, the body of Christ? Well, to help us think further, I would like to introduce the German sociologist Hartmut Rosa.

In the spring of 2023, I was in Tallin, Estonia, attending the General Assembly of the Conference of European Churches (which meets every five years and of which I was, at the time, vice president). The conference included a fine list of distinguished speakers, but the session that most left its mark on me was the one led by Professor Rosa.

I understand that he has quite a following in mainland Europe, where he undoubtedly speaks with a prophetic voice, but for some reason his message has not travelled to any great extent across the waters to Britain and he is a less well-known name here (in church circles at least). During the session in Tallin, Hartmut Rosa presented us with a picture of the ideologies that have shaped the capitalism of Western democracies. He demonstrated how they are predicated – both internally within Europe and when set against other world powers – on the notions of progress and growth, aggressive competition, dominance and power.

'Resonance spaces'

To succeed in the kind of environment this creates, businesses and organisations cannot simply keep pace with their competitors; they must prove themselves ahead of the game, growing, innovating and modernising at all costs. In the process, Rosa argues, the planet is being destroyed. Individuals are being crushed by unbearable and unreasonable pressures as the drive to succeed impacts our mental health, leading to depression and burn-out, to the detriment of society. The entire model is unsustainable, yet what is the alternative? Professor Rosa advocates that instead of struggling to keep pace, we should develop a model based on what he calls 'resonance'. This relates to a space in which to engage with others whose ideas are different, to learn and adapt, to reflect and appreciate, to connect more deeply and allow for the possibility of transformation. In his lecture, he suggested that Christianity already has such spaces, or at least strives to provide them, and that is why wider society still so desperately needs the Church. In such spaces we can pause, slow down and listen to God and one another.

As I mentioned, Hartmut Rosa is by profession a sociologist, but for me he speaks with theological depth, clarity and urgency. As he described the concept of 'resonance spaces', I felt huge relief and a sense of hope. I heard him remind the Church of her vocation, not to be large and successful, not to be anxious about the future, not to heap pressure on clergy and congregations to grow and increase in size, but simply to be a place where all are welcome; where we gather as the body of Christ, to pray, worship and serve our local communities; to learn and be shaped by one another. In resonance spaces we can cultivate the art of silence, learn to live less anxious lives, engage together in exploring the 'silences of the Bible'[6] – those unanswered questions that invite us to step deeper into our understanding of God's love, justice, judgement and mercy. In resonant spaces, we can face up to what Diarmaid MacCulloch calls 'bad silences',[7] bringing into the light those things that have been hidden in darkness and which the Church should address and repent of: involvement in the slave trade, sexual abuse, anti-Jewish rhetoric and discrimination against women, LGBTQI+ people and others.

Rosa issued a further challenge. If we are truly to be places of resonance, then we must avoid trying to predict what will emerge and how God might lead us: 'If the Church believes that it always knows what is right and what should come out of it, then it is no longer a resonance institution, but a resonance killer.'[8]

Strong words indeed, but ones that should sound a warning bell, reminding us that the future of the Church is in God's hands and we cannot control the outcome, however hard we plan and work. Instead, we are called to listen together for the whisper of the Holy Spirit and discern the next step of the journey; to hear God's still small voice saying something to us about being a new kind of community during a season in which we are smaller, less influential and more marginal. In response, I find myself asking, in the current drive towards an agenda of church growth and amid all the anxiety swirling around about future sustainability, might we be missing something essential about our Christian identity and call? Can we encourage our local churches to be places of resonance where the weary find rest and refreshment?

Embracing our weakness

In ending on the threshold of a question, I invite you into a space in which answers might be explored. And as I do so, I leave you with thoughts of two things. The first is an illustration and a reminder that God works through our frailties and vulnerabilities. My eldest son is a cellist, and a few years ago he had an accident with his beloved instrument. He bent over to pick it up from the floor where it was resting on its side and his phone fell out of his top pocket, puncturing a hole into the rib of the cello. It was, to put it mildly, a stressful evening in our home, but eventually the cello was taken to our trusted luthier, Clive, who had to remove the whole of the front of the instrument to be able to make the necessary repair. Over the course of several weeks, the cello underwent the equivalent of open heart surgery and through intricate and incredibly skilful work is now healthy and producing beautiful music again. But when we went to collect it, I learned something I didn't know before. As he handed the instrument over, Clive said, 'And I've made sure the mouse is back in the cello.' It turns out that many old stringed instruments have in them what they call in the trade a mouse, and if the front comes off, it is often carefully returned. The mouse is a dust ball, the accumulation of dirt collected over many years; the blood, sweat and tears of the player, and the gunk of everyday living. Rather than being removed or cleaned up, it is left in place as part of the story of the instrument.

I offer this enchanting image as encouragement. While seeking every day to become Christ-like, we are perhaps, like the cello, intended to embrace our weaknesses, to accept our shortcomings – our grubbiness even, if I can put it like that – and to be gentle and forgiving towards one another. God does not expect us to be shiny and shimmering, but to be dusty and imperfect, each with our own mouse, striving to make the kind of music that draws others closer to God.

And finally, some words of St David who, in his last recorded sermon, is reputed to have said that all that is required of us is to be joyful, keep the faith and do the little things well.[9] That is how light continues to shine; that is how spaces keep resonating with God's love.

Bach: Partita for Solo Violin

Looking for a musical evocation of the themes of light and space, there is no better place to turn to than the master of them all, J. S. Bach. There are so many great works, so much choice, but I've opted in the end for his Partita for Solo Violin No. 2 in D minor, and my favourite recording with the Israeli-American virtuoso violinist, Itzhak Perlman.[10]

The piece is around thirty minutes long, with the fifth and final crowning movement, Chaconne, lasting for half that time. If you only listen to part of the Partita, make sure it is the Chaconne, which the American violinist Joshua Bell has called 'not just one of the greatest pieces of music ever written, but one of the greatest achievements of any man [sic.] in history. It's a spiritually powerful piece, emotionally powerful, structurally perfect.'[11] With its technical demands and emotional scope, the Partita, and the Chaconne in particular, is an astonishing tour de force that is passionate, sensitive and thoughtful, even as it is exciting and thrilling. I know of no better piece that captures both the searing pain and exquisite joy of the human condition, creating a soundscape that seems to conjure the light and space of eternity.

For reflection

1 'And when music, as an art form, is experienced in real time ...' Think about an occasion when you took part in a performance or attended a concert. How did this differ from listening to a studio recording of the same piece(s)?

2 How might you create 'resonance spaces' in your home, church or neighbourhood to help others find understanding, rest or reconciliation?

3 As this book draws to a close, do you have a greater sense of the enduring melodies that sustain you? How will you ensure you keep listening to the music of the soul?

Epilogue

This book started with Mary and her song, the Magnificat. I'd like to end it with Mary too.

When I began in my role as Bishop of Chelmsford in the spring of 2021, I quickly became aware of the magnitude of all that was facing me. Along with the rest of the world, this vast and diverse diocese was emerging from the Covid pandemic. I was detecting high levels of exhaustion, with subtle overtones of disillusionment, and on top of that we were staring into the barrel of eyewatering financial challenges. Aware of my own inadequacy and sensing the weight of expectations, I felt utterly overwhelmed at times.

One day I chanced upon a painting on the internet called *Mary, Undoer of Knots* by the German artist Schmidtner.[1] In the baroque style, and dating from around the year 1700, the painting is apparently still on display at St Peter am Perlach Church in Augsburg, Bavaria. I confess I did not warm to the image, with its ornate and sentimentalised style and with the figure of Jesus notably absent. Nonetheless, I was immediately captivated by the title, which reminded me of my own dear mother, who was patience and grace personified, whether literally untying the knots of my childhood shoes or facing the challenges of life. She exuded a deep sense of trust and joy, carried her sorrows lightly and seldom showed signs of anxiety or worry.

Epilogue

Having developed links with the Orthodox monastery of St John the Baptist in Tolleshunt Knights, Essex, I asked Sr Gabriella, an experienced and devoted iconographer, to write an icon for me of *Mary, Undoer of Knots* in the traditional Eastern Orthodox style. And that's how the small but beautiful and precious icon, a labour of love, comes to hang in the chapel where I pray and spend time in silence each morning. Whatever our relationship with Mary, she 'always brings us to her son',[2] and in this icon the Christ child sits on his mother's lap. As Mary patiently unties one knot after another, the rope passes through his hands too.

Each day, when I gaze on the icon, I'm encouraged and reminded that in the Diocese of Chelmsford, as in life, we need only face one knot at a time. As in my icon, loose threads remain – those ragged strands that will never be entirely tidied up or incorporated neatly into the woven rope – but they too are beautiful and add character as part of the rich tapestry of our lives.

So, as I strain to hear the music of the soul, I do so with thanksgiving for all that has been, and with a sense of peace I reach out towards what is yet to come.

Notes

Introduction

1 Michael Mayne, *The Enduring Melody* (London: Darton, Longman & Todd Ltd, 2006).

2 A version with shortened musical excerpts can be found on BBC Sounds: https://www.bbc.co.uk/sounds/play/m001vbq7 (accessed 12 March 2025).

I The Magnificat

1 Tom Holland, *Dominion: The making of the Western mind* (Boston: Little, Brown and Company, 2019).

2 Tom Holland, 'How religion shaped politics and the Western world', episode 52, *The Rest Is Politics (Leading)*, 25 December 2023. Available as a podcast at: https://www.audible.co.uk/podcast/52-Tom-Holland-How-religion-shaped-politics-and-the-Western-world/B0CQWLCBK (accessed 12 March 2025).

3 Christopher Cocksworth, *Mary: Bearer of life* (London: SCM Press, 2023), p. 3.

4 Cocksworth, *Mary: Bearer of life*, p. 3.

5 See David Wynne's Madonna in Ely Cathedral at: https://www.elycathedral.org/about/history-heritage/the-lady-chapel (accessed 12 March 2025).

6 I have written more fully about the Anglican Church in Iran and its impact and influence on my life in an earlier book, *Cries for a Lost Homeland: Reflections on*

Jesus' sayings from the Cross (Norwich: Canterbury Press, 2021).

7 Pergolesi, *Stabat Mater,* with Nathalie Stutzmann conducting the Orfeo 55 ensemble, and soloists Philippe Jaroussky and Emöke Barath, recorded at the Château de Fontainebleau, France, April 2014. Video by Ozango / ARTE France: https://www.youtube.com/watch?v=qzOmPUu-F_M (accessed 12 March 2025).

For a guide to Pergolesi's *Stabat Mater* see, for example, Kate Bolton-Porciatti, 'Pergolesi's *Stabat Mater*: a guide to the composer's masterpiece and its best recording', 8 July 2022, in the BBC's Classical Music Magazine: https://www.classical-music.com/features/recordings/pergolesis-stabat-mater-a-guide-to-the-composers-masterpiece-and-its-best-recordings (accessed 12 March 2025).

2 Flight

1 William Boyd, *Ordinary Thunderstorms* (London: Bloomsbury, 2009).

2 Steve Taylor, *Extraordinary Awakenings: From trauma to transformation* (Novato, CA: New World Library, 2021).

3 The album *Say Your Most Beautiful Word,* by Mahan Mirarab, was released in 2022. The following link provides details and includes a recording of the track of the same name, together with an English translation of Shamloo's poem: https://mahanmirarab.bandcamp.com/track/say-your-most-beautiful-word (accessed 13 March 2025).

3 Violence

1 Guli Francis-Dehqani, *Cries for a Lost Homeland: Reflections on Jesus' sayings from the Cross* (Norwich: Canterbury Press, 2021).

2 For more on the Church in Iran and the impact of the Islamic Revolution, see also two books written by my late father, Hassan Dehqani-Tafti: *The Hard Awakening* (London: SPCK, 1981) and *Unfolding Design of My World: A pilgrim in exile* (Norwich: Canterbury Press, 2000).

3 Hannah Arendt, *The Human Condition* (Chicago: University of Chicago Press, 1998).

4 Sarah Perry, *Enlightenment* (London: Penguin, 2025).

5 'Sarah Perry: The Waterstones Interview', https://www.youtube.com/watch?v=ywCQHUeIP3M (accessed 30 May 2025).

6 This is a link to the recording of 'Variations on Bahram's Melody' used on *Desert Island Discs*: https://www.youtube.com/watch?v=__IfyN9zZ8c (accessed 14 March 2025). The musicians are Fiona Sweeney (flute), Kryštof Kohout (violin), Gabriel Francis-Dehqani (cello) and Will Harmer (piano). *Hymns Persian and English, with words and tunes in common* is a compilation of fifty-seven hymns from the Persian Hymnal, together with music and English translations, including Bahram's melody. Copies are available online from Elam Ministries bookshop, Kalameh: https://shop.kalameh.com/english_store_view/common-hymns-in-english-and-persian-with-music.html (accessed 14 March 2025). *39 Persian Hymns, with music* is a compilation

of thirty-nine Persian hymns, available online, together
with a CD recording, from Elam Ministries bookshop,
Kalameh: https://shop.kalameh.com/english_store_view/
music/39-persian-hymns-with-cd.html (accessed 14
March 2025).

4 Angels

1 Elizabeth Laird, with illustrations by Battina Paterson,
Gabriel's Feather (Pittsburgh, PA: Scholastica, 1998).
2 Nick Cave and Sean O'Hagan, *Faith, Hope and Carnage*
(Edinburgh: Canongate Books, 2023).
3 *The Boatman's Call* is the tenth studio album by Nick Cave
and the Bad Seeds and was released in 1997.
4 Cave and O'Hagan, *Faith, Hope and Carnage*, p. 51.

5 Fear and hope

1 For more on Vaclav Havel's thinking and writing on the
theme of hope, see, for example, Tara C. Trapani, 'Vaclav
Havel on Hope', Yale Forum on Religion and Ecology, 24
August 2023: https://fore.yale.edu/blogs/entry/1692889095
(accessed 14 March 2025).
2 Václav Havel, *Disturbing the Peace* (London: Vintage, 1991).
3 https://fore.yale.edu/blogs/entry/1692889095 (accessed 14
March 2025).

6 Reconciliation

1 For more about the work of Musalaha see, for example,
Salim Munayer (ed.), *Journey through the Storm: Lessons
from Lusalaha, Ministry of Reconciliation* (Cumbria:
Langham Global Library, 2020).

2 Programme notes for a performance of Benjamin Britten's *War Requiem*. Prom 37, 17 August 2024.

3 Read more on this at: https://mediacentre.christianaid. org.uk/childrens-letters-from-gaza-handed-to-new-pm-asking-why-must-we-pay-such-a-horrendous-price/ (accessed 15 March 2025).

4 David Runcorn, *The Language of Tears: Their gift, mystery and meaning* (Norwich: Canterbury Press, 2018).

5 Runcorn, *The Language of Tears*, p. 2.

6 There is a brief write-up about the museum and the story behind it on the website of Article 18, a human rights organisation dedicated to the protection and promotion of religious freedom in Iran, which includes a link to the forty-four-second promotional video: https:// articleeighteen.com/news/10530/ (accessed 15 March 2025).

7 Runcorn, *The Language of Tears*, pp. 83–4.

8 Allyson McCabe, *Why Sinéad O'Connor Matters* (Austin, TX: University of Texas Press, 2023).

7 Silence and darkness

1 R. S. Thomas, 'Kneeling'. See: https://www. poetryfoundation.org/poems/48946/kneeling-56d22a97b5917 (accessed 26 March 2025).

2 Silvianne and Barnabas Aspray, 'The questions that nobody can escape' in *Seen & Unseen*, 22 August 2024: https://www.seenandunseen.com/questions-nobody-can-escape (accessed 17 March 2025).

3 Evelyn Underhill, adapted by Robyn Wrigley Carr in *Music of Eternity: Meditations for Advent with Evelyn*

Underhill (London: SPCK, 2001), p. 69. Original text in *The Life of the Spirit and the Life of Today*, a series of lectures delivered in Oxford in 1921 (London: Mowbray, 1922).

4 Barbara Brown Taylor, *Learning to Walk in the Dark* (Norwich: Canterbury Press, 2015).

5 There are many fine recordings of Dvořák's cello concerto available but, for me, the great Mstislav Rostropovich, together with conductor Herbert von Karajan and the Berlin Philharmonic, provides the definitive version. It is older than many recordings, but difficult to surpass, both in the warmth of its ambience and its sublime and expressive beauty. It is available on CD (Deutsche Grammophon, 1969).

8 Light and space

1 The stained glass window was designed in 2023 by Elspeth Manders.

2 Guli Francis-Dehquai, *Cries for a Lost Homeland: Reflections on Jesus' sayings from the Cross* (Norwich: Canterbury Press, 2021), pp. 11–19.

3 This quote is from Christopher Cocksworth, *Mary: Bearer of life* (London: SCM, 2023), p. 74.

4 Antony Gormley, 'Art, religion, and the battle for culture', episode 66, *The Rest Is Politics (Leading)*, 25 March 2024. Available as a podcast.

5 Belle Tindall, 'The poem became flesh and dwelt among us', in *Seen & Unseen*, 1 December 2023: https://www.seenandunseen.com/poem-became-flesh-and-dwelt-among-us (accessed 19 March 2025).

6 K. H. Ting writes about the importance of paying attention to what the Bible does not say, as well as what it does say. See K. H. Ting, 'A Chinese Example: "The silences of the Bible", in R. S. Sugirtharajah (ed.), *Voices from the Margin: Interpreting the Bible in the Third World* (London: SPCK), pp. 431–33.

7 Diarmaid MacCulloch, 'Good Silence, Bad Silence', episode 5 of Radio 4's *The Essay: Talking about silence,* 14 April 2022; available on BBC Sounds.

8 Hartmut Rosa, 'Being European – a Sociological Assessment: 2023 and Beyond', an address given at the General Assembly of the Conference of European Churches, Tallin, Estonia, 16 June 2023. See also Hartmut Rosa, *Resonance: A sociology of our relationship to the world*, trans. James C. Wagner (Cambridge: Polity Press, 2019) and Hartmut Rosa, *Social Acceleration: A new theory of modernity* (New York: Columbia University Press, 2013).

9 See, for example, Andrew Brookes O.P., 'St David, Patron of Wales', 1 March 2013: https://www.english.op.org/godzdogz/st-david-patron-of-wales/ (accessed 19 March 2025).

10 Partita for Solo Violin No. 2 in D Minor, BWV 1004, on *J. S. Bach Sonatas and Partitas* with violinist Itzhak Perlman (Warner Classics, 2 CD pack, released in 2015).

11 Joshua Bell, quoted in Wikipedia: https://en.wikipedia.org/wiki/Partita_for_Violin_No._2_(Bach) (accessed 19 March 2025).

Epilogue

1 To view the image and learn more about the story behind it, see https://ewtn.no/the-remarkable-story-behind-mary-undoer-of-knots-will-give-you-faith-through-the-impossible/ (accessed 19 March 2025).

2 Pope Francis, quoted in Christopher Cocksworth, *Mary: Bearer of life* (London: SCM, 2023), p. 4.